THE THINGS WE COOK.

A GREEN HOPE FARM COOKBOOK
WRITTEN by MOLLY SHEEHAN
ILLUSTRATED by Alli HOWE

THE THINGS WE COOK
A GREEN HOPE FARM
COOKbooK.

WRITTEN by Molly SHEEHAN
illUSTRATED by Alli HOWE

Copyright Molly SHEEHAN
2013

ISBN: 978-1-4675-9031-0

FIRST PRINTING: FALL 2013

PUbliSHED by GREEN HOPE FARM
PRESS
P.O. BOX 125
MERIDEN, NH
03770

COVER DESIGN by Alli HOWE

THANKS TO MEHER BABA AND MEHERA FOR EVERYTHING.

THANKS TO DEAR JIM FOR EVERY SINGLE NAIL YOU HAVE HAMMERED INTO PLACE TO MAKE THE DREAM OF GREEN HOPE FARM INTO A REALITY.

THANKS TO BEN, ELIZABETH, EMILY AND WILLIAM FOR CHEERFULLY EATING WHATEVER I'VE COOKED FOR YOU, AND IN BETWEEN MEALS, EMBRACING THE ADVENTURE OF GREEN HOPE FARM WITH OPEN HEARTS AND A SENSE OF HUMOR.

TO GRACE FOR BEING THE FIRST IN A NEW GENERATION.

THANKS TO STAFF GODDESS AND ARTIST EXTRAORDINAIRE Alli HOWE. THIS COOKBOOK TURNED OUT A THOUSAND TIMES BETTER THAN ANYTHING I COULD HAVE IMAGINED BECAUSE OF YOU.

FINAllY, THANKS TO EVERYONE WHO HAS BEEN A PART OF THIS FARM BE THEY ANIMAL, PERSON, ANGEL, NATURE SPIRIT OR FLOWER.

—MOlly SHEEHAN.

For family, friends and all others who will enjoy this cookbook. No matter who you are, I hope you see this cookbook as a gift from a friend.

Thanks to Molly. Without her I would never have had this delicious material to illustrate!

To my mom for being so supportive in my time of transition, love you more.

And lastly... For sweet ♡ olive.

— Alli Howe

LIFE BRINGS SO MANY MOMENTS TO CELE-
BRATE AND ON A FARM, THERE ARE ALWAYS
FLOWERS AND FOOD TO ADD TO THE JOY. HERE
AT GREEN HOPE FARM, WHEN ANY BELOVED
HAS SOMETHING TO SHOUT ABOUT, WE COOK UP A
MEAL TOGETHER WITH BOUNTY FROM OUR GARDENS.

IN THIS COOKBOOK WE SHARE WITH YOU OUR
FAVORITE RECIPES FOR ALL THINGS COOKED AND
EATEN AT GREEN HOPE FARM GATHERINGS,
LARGE AND SMALL.

IT'S WITH MUCH DELIGHT AND GRATITUDE TO
EVERYONE WHO HAS EVER BEEN PART OF GREEN
HOPE FARM THAT I SHARE THIS COOKBOOK WITH
YOU! I HOPE YOU LOVE THIS COOKBOOK AS
MUCH AS WE HAVE LOVED CREATING IT FOR
YOU!

— MOLLY SHEEHAN, GREEN HOPE FARM,
   FALL 2013

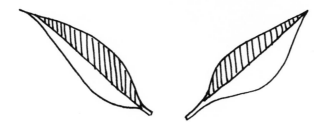

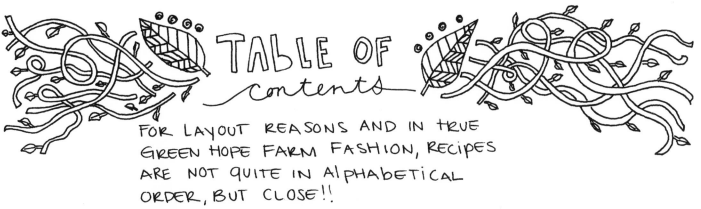

TABLE OF *contents*

FOR LAYOUT REASONS AND IN TRUE
GREEN HOPE FARM FASHION, RECIPES
ARE NOT QUITE IN ALPHABETICAL
ORDER, BUT CLOSE!!

MAIN DISHES

EXTRAS:

A BRIEF HISTORY OF GREEN HOPE FARM

THE BEST MOMENTS OF MY CHILDHOOD WERE SPENT PLAYING IN THE WOODS, PUTTERING AROUND IN BOATS ON THE POND IN MY BACKYARD, AND WHEN RAIN PREVAILED, READING BOOKS LIKE "A SECRET GARDEN" by FRANCES BURNETT HODGES AND "OLD TIME FAIRY TALES" by KATHARINE LEE BATES. GIVEN MY LOVE FOR NATURE, FOR FLOWERS IN PARTICULAR, AND ALWAYS FOR THE FAIRIES, IT SHOULD COME AS NO SURPRISE THAT WHEN IT CAME TO CREATING GREEN HOPE FARM MY PARTNERS INCLUDED ANGELS AND NATURE SPIRITS. THANK GOD FOR THESE FRIENDS AS I HAVE NEEDED THEIR SUPERIOR EXPERTISE ABOUT ALL THINGS IN THE GARDEN AND ALL THINGS TO DO WITH RUNNING A BUSTLING FARM BUSINESS.

WITH NO IDEA WHAT AN ADVENTURE LAY AHEAD, MY HUSBAND JIM AND I FOUND THE LAND FOR OUR FARM ALMOST THIRTY YEARS AGO. ON A BEAUTIFUL HILLTOP WITH A SOUTH SLOPING MEADOW BENEATH OUR FEET, WE BUILT OUR FARMHOUSE AS A PLACE TO RAISE OUR FOUR CHILDREN - BEN, ELIZABETH, EMILY AND WILLIAM. WHILE JIM TOOK ON THE HERCULEAN TASK OF BUILDING OUR HOME AND ALL THE OUTBUILDINGS FOR AN EVER-EXPANDING FARM, I TOOK ON THE GARDENS. I PLANTED AN ORCHARD AND A PATCH OF MANY KINDS OF BERRIES. I ENCIRCLED THE HOUSE IN FLOWER GARDENS. I PLANTED TREES AND SHRUBS, PARTICULARLY ROSES. I CREATED VEGETABLE GARDENS. A LOT OF THEM. WE GOT CHICKENS, DOGS, CATS AND HONEYBEES. FARMING WAS THE LIFE I ALWAYS WANTED, AND I WAS THRILLED TO BE LIVING MY DREAM.

ALMOST IMMEDIATELY GREEN HOPE FARM TOOK ON A LIFE OF ITS OWN. GREEN HOPE FARM'S ANGELIC PARTNERS SUGGESTED I MAKE VIBRATIONAL REMEDIES CALLED FLOWER ESSENCES FROM OUR ORGANICALLY GROWN FLOWERS. MUCH TO MY SURPRISE, THIS PROJECT GREW RAPIDLY INTO A MAIL ORDER BUSINESS THAT NOW SHARES FLOWER ESSENCES WITH PEOPLE AND ANIMALS ALL OVER THE EARTH. A PLACE OF HEALING FOR OUR FAMILY UNEXPECTEDLY BECAME A PLACE TO HELP OTHERS IN THEIR OWN HEALING JOURNEYS. AS WE GREW, WE BLOSSOMED INTO A COMMUNITY OF PEOPLE WORKING IN THE GARDENS AND SHIPPING OUR FLOWER ESSENCES TO BELOVEDS EVERYWHERE. FORTUNATELY FOR US, THIS PRECIOUS STAFF HAS ALWAYS INCLUDED MARVELOUS COOKS WHOSE RECIPES ARE INCLUDED HERE.

P.S. IF YOU'D LIKE TO KNOW MORE ABOUT GREEN HOPE FARM AND GREEN HOPE FARM FLOWER ESSENCES AND HOW THEY MIGHT SERVE YOU AND THE ANIMALS IN YOUR LIFE, CHECK OUT OUR WEBSITE: WWW.greenhopeessences.com OR E-MAIL US AT GREEN.HOPE.farm@valley.net

My life has been filled with amazing cooks, but this cookbook would not be complete without describing the three cooks that have taught me the most: My wonderful grandmother Kitty, my beloved friend and neighbor Teddy, and my son, Ben, kitchen wizard.

My Grandmother

BORN IN ST. LOUIS, MISSOURI, ON AUGUST 11, 1907, MY DARLING GRANDMOTHER, KATHARINE SALMON, WAS ALWAYS CALLED KITTY. IN THE CIVIL WAR, ONE OF HER GRANDFATHERS FOUGHT FOR THE UNION AND THE OTHER ONE FOR THE CONFEDERACY, NOT AN UNUSUAL THING IN THE MISSOURI OF HER DAY.

AS A LITTLE GIRL, KITTY BROKE HER ARM FALLING OFF A SIDEWALK PLAYING JACKS. THE DOCTOR SET HER ARM WRONG, AND FROM THEN ON SHE COULDN'T TOUCH HER HAND TO HER SHOULDER. THIS DIDN'T STOP HER FROM BEING A FABULOUS ATHLETE ESPECIALLY ON THE BASKETBALL COURT. HER MOTHER'S FATHER WAS IN THE RAILROAD BUSINESS, A CIRCUMSTANCE THAT TOOK HER FAMILY TO SEATTLE AT THE END OF HER HIGH SCHOOL YEARS. THIS BECAME THE CITY SHE THOUGHT OF AS HOME.

DESPITE HER LOVE FOR THE PACIFIC NORTHWEST, KITTY WENT EAST TO COLLEGE. SHE TOOK THE TRAIN ACROSS COUNTRY EACH SEPTEMBER IN AN UNCHAPERONED TRAVELING PARTY OF FELLOW COLLEGE STUDENTS, DANCING THE CHARLESTON ALL THE WAY FROM COAST TO COAST. A SOCIAL WHIRL ALSO ENVELOPED HER DURING HER SUMMERS IN SEATTLE. ONE SEASON SHE AND HER BEST FRIENDS, BOBBY AND GLEN, VOWED TO MAKE THE SOCIETY PAGES EVERY DAY ALL SUMMER. THEY PULLED IT OFF BY HAVING A SMALL FENDER BENDER ON THE ONE DAY THERE WAS NO SOCIETY EVENT.

WHEN KITTY MARRIED A MAN FROM THE EAST, HER HOMETOWN BOYFRIEND BURNED HER LETTERS UNDER A STREET LAMP BENEATH HER BEDROOM WINDOW THE NIGHT BEFORE HER WEDDING. AS A LITTLE GIRL, I THOUGHT THIS A MOST ROMANTIC STORY, SOMEHOW IDENTIFYING MOST MOST WITH THE SORROW OF THE FORMER BEAU. AS A YOUNG MOTHER KITTY LIVED IN PARIS

SHE WROTE A DETECTIVE STORY SET IN THIS CITY CALLED "I'M AFRAID I'LL LIVE." APPARENTLY IT WAS SUCH A RISQUE TALE THAT A) HER GRANDCHILDREN WERE NOT ALLOWED TO READ IT, AND B) SHE HAD TO PUBLISH IT UNDER A PSEUDONYM TO PROTECT MY GRANDFATHER'S CAREER.

IN A WORLDLY SENSE, MY GRANDFATHER DID HAVE A BRILLIANT CAREER. THIS MEANT MY GRANDMOTHER'S JOB BECAME THAT OF HOSTESS. I NEVER HEARD HER COMPLAIN ABOUT THIS, THOUGH I IMAGINE IT HAD ITS UPS AND DOWNS. THE ONE PAINFUL THING SHE DID MENTION WAS THAT HER HAIR WENT WHITE WHEN SHE WAS ONLY TWENTY-FIVE. SHE HAD BEEN CONSIDERED A BEAUTY UNTIL THEN BUT, AFTERWARDS, SOME PEOPLE SOMETIMES THOUGHT SHE WAS THE MOTHER OF HER HUSBAND. WHEN I ASKED HER WHY SHE HADN'T DYED HER HAIR, SHE SAID THE DYES WERE VERY STRANGE IN HER DAY AND DIDN'T WORK WELL WITH HER HAIR.

KITTY WAS A MAVERICK, AND SHE WAS OPEN MINDED ABOUT ALL KINDS OF THINGS. AT HER 60TH BIRTHDAY PARTY IN 1947, SHE ASKED EVERYONE TO DRESS UP IN THE FASHIONS OF THE DAY. HER OWN OUTFIT WAS A PSYCHEDELIC PRINT MINI SKIRT, ENORMOUS SUNGLASSES, A PINK WIG AND GO GO BOOTS. THAT SAME YEAR SHE GOT ALL OF US PAPER DRESSES FOR CHRISTMAS.

MY GRANDMOTHER'S SENSE OF MISCHIEF OFTEN SHOWED IN HER FOOD. AFTER ALL, FOOD HAD BECOME HER VENUE BY DEFAULT, SO SHE HAD FUN WITH IT. ONE CHRISTMAS DINNER SHE MADE JELLIED CONSOMME MADRILÈNE FOR THE FIRST COURSE. ALL HER GRANDCHILDREN THOUGHT OUR GOURMET GRANDMA HAD GONE ROGUE AND WAS ACTUALLY SERVING US JELLO! WE WERE THRILLED! SHE

THOUGHT IT WAS SO FUNNY WHEN WE All SPIT OUT OUR FIRST MOUTHFULS OF THE SALTY STUFF.

WHEN I WAS A CHILD, My FAMILY SPENT A LARGE CHUNK OF THE SUMMER WITH MY GRANDPARENTS AT AN OLD LOG CAMP IN THE ADIRONDACKS. THE PLACE WAS SIX MILES DOWN A LAKE FROM THE NEAREST ROAD. RESUPPLYING THE KITCHEN WAS A BIG PROJECT INVOLVING BOAT RIDES AND A LONG DRIVE TO A TINY TOWN WITH A VERY STRANGE SUPER-MARKET. PRODUCE WAS A PARTICULAR PROBLEM. WHEN VISITORS ARRIVED, THEIR OFFERINGS OF FRUITS AND VEGET-ABLES WERE OFTEN GREETED WITH MORE DELIGHT THAN THEY WERE, ESPECIALLY IF THEY HAD BROUGHT ADIRONDACK RARITIES LIKE RIPE TOMATOES OR FRESH CORN.

SINCE THE ADIRONDACKS IS A TEMPERATE RAIN FOREST THERE WERE MANY RAINY DAYS SPENT IN THE KITCHEN WITH KITTY. IN BETWEEN DISCUSSIONS OF WHAT COULD BE SCROUNGED TOGETHER FOR DINNER, SHE TAUGHT ME CARD GAMES LIKE RUSSIAN BANK. SHE ALSO LISTENED TO ME AS WE TALKED OF LIFE, DEATH AND IMMORTALITY. OUT ON THE PORCH, GENERATIONS OF MEN WOULD WAX POETIC ABOUT TROUT LANDED AND PONDS FISHED, WHILE IN THE KITCHEN, THE WOMEN MADE DO WITH MISMATCHED CHINA, PECULIAR UTENSILS AND WHATEVER STRANGE INGREDIENTS COULD BE TOSSED TOGETHER TO FORM A MEAL.

WE MIXED ODD THINGS TOGETHER BECAUSE NO MATTER HOW WELL WE PLANNED THINGS AHEAD, WE ALWAYS SEEMED TO RUN OUT OF KEY INGREDIENTS. CAKES WOULD HAVE TO BE BAKED WITHOUT THE RIGHT LEAVENING AGENTS OR FROSTED WITHOUT

CONFECTIONER'S SUGAR. SEVEN MINUTE ICING, BEATEN FOR A FULL SEVEN MINUTES, WAS OUR FALLBACK WHEN ONLY GRANULATED SUGAR WAS AVAILABLE. TO THIS DAY I REALLY DON'T LIKE SEVEN MINUTE ICING BECAUSE OF ALL THE TIMES I WAS THE ONE CRANED OVER THE STEAMING DOUBLE BOILER, BEATING THIS ICING WITH A ROTARY EGG BEATER.

ALL THE UNUSUAL SUBSTITUTIONS LED TO SOME WELL-REMEMBERED CULINARY HIGHS AND LOWS. WE NEVER QUITE MESSED UP AS BADLY AS MY GREAT GRAND-MOTHER WHO HAD TRIED TO GET THE FAMILY TO EAT HER HAND-CHURNED ICE CREAM THAT HAD KEROSENE SPILLED IN IT. BUT LET'S FACE IT, DOING BETTER THAN KEROSENE ICE CREAM DOESN'T EXACTLY SET THE BAR HIGH.

RECIPES WERE ALSO IN SHORT SUPPLY. THE CAMP HAD BUT ONE TATTERED COOKBOOK WITH AN OFT USED RECIPE FOR HUNGARIAN PLUM CAKE, WHATEVER THAT WAS! WE USED THIS RECIPE FOR BLUEBERRIES WE PICKED AS IT WAS THE CLOSEST THING WE HAD TO A BLUEBERRY CAKE RECIPE. I DON'T THINK WE EVER DID TRY THE RECIPE WITH PLUMS, BUT IT WORKED WONDERFULLY WELL WITH THOSE BLUEBERRIES! KITTY BROUGHT TO ALL THESE CULINARY QUANDARIES AND MISADVENTURES AN INFECTIOUS SENSE OF THE ABSURD.

NOT ALL MY GRANDMOTHER'S COOKING WAS SO HIT OR MISS AS DURING ADIRONDACK SUMMERS. KITTY ENTERTAINED LEGIONS OF MUCKETY MUCKS IN HER DAY AND KNEW A LOT OF GREAT RECIPES. ONE

YEAR FOR CHRISTMAS SHE COLLECTED ALL HER BEST RECIPES AND TYPED THEM UP FOR HE DAUGHTERS, CALLING THE COLLECTION, "THE COPY CAT COOKBOOK". SINCE THEN, I HAVE DONE THREE MORE EDITIONS OF "THE COPY CAT COOKBOOK". MANY OF THE RECIPES IN THIS BOOK COME RIGHT FROM THESE COOKBOOKS. IN KITTY'S "COPY CAT COOKBOOK" SHE INCLUDED A RECIPE FOR A HORRIBLE DESSERT CALLED "EMERGENCY PUDDING". SHE HAD MADE THIS DISH TO MUCH CRITICISM WHEN, DURING WORLD WAR II, SHE WAS EXPECTED TO PRODUCE A MEAL FOR COMPANY ON SHORT NOTICE. I LIKED THAT SASS- TO SLIP IN HER WORST RECIPE ALONG WITH ALL THE BEST.

I TREASURED MY GRANDMOTHER'S SUBVERSIVE ATTITUDE. THERE WERE A LOT OF NARROW MINDED, RIGHTEOUS FOLK IN MY FAMILY, AND SHE ENCOURAGED ME TO GO MY OWN WAY AND TRUST MY OWN HEART. MY SENSE OF SELF AND SENSE OF VALUE CAME FROM HER SEEING AND ACKNOWLEDGING SOMETHING IN ME THAT HADN'T MET THE APPROVAL OF THE WORLD OR MY PARENTS. SHE GOT ME THROUGH MY CHILDHOOD.

TEDDY

TEDDY KNEW HOW TO MAKE AN ENTRANCE. YES, IT HELPED THAT SHE ALWAYS ARRIVED AT ANY EVENT BEARING A GLORIOUS PLATTER OF GOURMET GOODNESS, BUT HER SWIRLING COATS, WONDERFUL PERFUME, COTERIE OF MINIATURE FRENCH POODLES AND GENERAL JE NE SAIS QUOI SEALED THE DEAL. EVERYONE KNEW WHEN TEDDY HAD ARRIVED!

WHEN TEDDY AND I FIRST MET, I COULD ONLY WONDER WHAT THIS GLAMOROUS WOMAN WAS DOING ON A FARM IN THE HILLS OF NEW HAMPSHIRE. WELL, SHE WAS BUSY FARMING FOR ONE THING. OFTEN I WOULD SEE HER ROARING THROUGH OUR TINY VILLAGE IN WHAT WE CAME TO CALL HER "STAFF CAR", A BLACK DIESEL MERCEDES BENZ SEDAN, WITH SOME GLORIOUS SCARF WRAPPED AROUND HER NECK AND A TREE COMING OUT OF THE TRUNK.

WITHIN MINUTES OF BEING INTRODUCED, TEDDY TOOK ME INTO A FIELD TO DIG JERUSALEM ARTICHOKES. SHE WAS A GRANDMOTHER WITH A NEW HIP, BUT NOTHING SEEMED TO SLOW HER DOWN. WE DUG TUBERS FOR A FEW HOURS, RELISHING THE FACT WE WERE KINDRED SPIRITS WHO HAD FOUND EACH OTHER. AND THEN WHEN WE HAD DUG ENOUGH FOR A LONG WINTER, THERE WAS A YUMMY TEDDY SNACK WAITING IN HER KITCHEN.

TEDDY TOOK ME UNDER HER WING — WHICH WAS A VERY FUN PLACE TO BE. WE HAD ADVENTURES WITH A CAPITAL "A". SHE THOUGHT NOTHING OF LOADING UP THE STAFF CAR WITH MY LITTLE CHILDREN AND HER DOGS AND SETTING OFF TO COASTAL MAINE FOR THE DAY. HER FATHER HAD BEEN A GENTLEMAN FARMER WHO OWNED

THE PENINSULA OF WOLFE'S NECK IN CASCO BAY. TEDDY MISSED THAT FARM HER WHOLE LIFE, AND RETURNING THERE WAS HER FAVORITE ADVENTURE.

WELL, OTHER THAN JAUNTS TO FRANCE. HER FATHER LOST HIS MONEY IN THE GREAT DEPRESSION. TEDDY WORKED HER WHOLE LIFE AS A NURSE, but SHE LIVED AS IF THE SHIP HAD NEVER BEEN LOST. SHE WOULD DASH OFF TO SOUTHERN FRANCE WITH A FRIEND, BRINGING NOTHING MORE THAN A WELL-STOCKED PURSE, A SILK blOUSE AND AN ULTRA SUEDE SKIRT. SHE ALWAYS LOOKED ELEGANT, AS CHIC AS ANY FRENCH-WOMAN.

I SPENT WHAT FELT LIKE A MILLION HOURS SITTING ON HER WINDOW SEAT IN HER SNUG LITTLE FARM HOUSE EATING AMAZING FOOD, SIPPING TEA AND LOOKING AT THE FIELD NEXT DOOR. TEDDY WOULD ENCOURAGE MY KIDS AND HER GRANDCHILDREN TO DRESS UP, TAKE bubblE bATHS, WELCOME THE DOGS INTO THE bubblE bATHS, COOK TREATS WITH HER, CRANK UP THE OLD MUSIC bOX AND DANCE. THOSE VISITS bECAME blISS-FULLY EASIER WHEN WE built OUR FARMHOUSE ON THAT VERY FIELD NEXT DOOR.

WAY BEFORE ANYONE ELSE I KNEW WAS INTO EXOTIC BRANDS OF ANYTHING, TEDDY'S PANTRY WAS A WONDERLAND OF ENGLISH JAMS, FRENCH CHEESES MOROCCAN SPICES, HAWAIIAN GUAVA PASTE AND PRODUCE FROM HER OWN LAVISH GARDENS.

HER PARTIES WERE LEGEND. HER FIRST HUSBAND HAD BEEN IN THE NAVY, AND TEDDY HAD BEEN POSTED WITH HIM TO BRAZIL, HAWAII AND PORTUGAL AMONG OTHER PLACES. SHE HAD AN ENORMOUS LONG TABLE FROM THE PORTUGAL YEARS THAT SHE WOULD COVER IN WONDROUS FOODS. HER PAELLA WAS MORE LOBSTER THAN RICE. PEOPLE FOUGHT OVER HER CREAM PUFFS. MORNING, NOON OR NIGHT THERE WAS ALWAYS SOMETHING THAT HAD BEEN BAKED FOR COMPANY. TEDDY AND HER SECOND HUSBAND, MALCOLM, LOVED TO MAKE NEW FRIENDS, AND EVERYONE WAS INVITED OVER FOR A MEAL.

MALCOLM WAS AN ORDAINED MINISTER WHO FELT HIS MISSION WAS WITH THOSE WHO HAD NO CHURCH. HE WOULD MARRY AND BURY THOSE WHO BELONGED TO NO CONGREGATION OR THOSE WHOSE FAITH WAS "OUTSIDE THE BOX". HIS CEREMONIES WERE WONDERFULLY PERSONAL AS HE SPENT MUCH TIME GETTING TO KNOW ALL THE PLAYERS BEFORE ANY EVENT HE OFFICIATED. TEDDY COULD BE COUNTED ON TO OFFER UP A HOMEMADE DANISH OR BLUEBERRY BUCKLE RIGHT FROM THE OVEN TO THE FAMILIES AS THEY MADE THEIR WEDDING PLANS WITH MALCOLM.

JIM AND I WERE ONCE INVITED TO ONE OF TEDDY'S PARTIES WHEN THE GUEST LIST WAS FOLKS MALCOLM HAD MARRIED. WE WERE THE ONE EXCEPTION AS WE COULD ONLY WISH WE HAD KNOWN MALCOLM WHEN WE WERE MARRIED. AT THIS PARTY I MET LYNN TIDMAN. SHE WENT ON TO WRITE OUR FLOWER ESSENCE LABELS FOR

TWENTY YEARS. I ALSO MET JAYN BIER WHO HELPED ME SO MUCH IN THE GREENHOUSE AND OUT IN THE ROSE GARDEN. TEDDY AND MALCOLM ATTRACTED WONDERFUL INTERESTING PEOPLE, AND THEY TOOK CARE OF THEM WELL.

I WAS A MORE CAUTIOUS COOK BEFORE I MET TEDDY, AND SHE SET ME FREE TO HAVE MUCH MORE FUN IN THE KITCHEN. SHE BECAME A REAL MOTHER TO ME AS WELL, AND THAT WAS HER MOST PRECIOUS GIFT.

ONE FINAL TEDDY STORY THAT I LOVE FOR ITS TWIST. TEDDY HAD A HALF SISTER WHO MADE AMAZING CARAMELS. SHE WAS FAMOUS FOR THESE CARAMELS AND WOULD NOT SHARE THE RECIPE WITH ANYONE. WHEN THIS HALF SISTER GOT VERY ILL, TEDDY DROPPED EVERYTHING TO GO NURSE HER AND DID SO UNTIL SHE DIED. WHEN SHE WAS GONE, TEDDY THOUGHT, "WELL FINALLY, I WILL FIND OUT HOW SHE MADE THOSE DARN CARAMELS!" WHEN SHE WENT TO HER HALF SISTER'S RECIPE BOOK, THE HALF SISTER HAD RIPPED OUT THE PAGE WHERE THE CARAMEL RECIPE HAD BEEN.

PERHAPS THIS WAS ONE REASON WHY TEDDY SHARED HER RECIPES WITH ANY AND ALL WHO ASKED. BUT PERHAPS IT WAS JUST BECAUSE TEDDY HAD A big GENEROUS HEART.

AS A SMALL BOY, BEN HAD ZERO
INTEREST IN FOOD. WHILE HE SOMETIMES
LIKED THE PROJECT OF COOKING, HE WAS
NOT INTERESTED IN SAMPLING THE RESULTS.
HE ATE TO LIVE AND WITH A LACK OF
ENTHUSIASM. THAT MADE ME THINK HE WOULD
ALWAYS BE LIKE THIS. WHAT A SURPRISE WHEN
HE BECAME THE BEST COOK IN OUR FAMILY.

THE CHILD WHO HAD EATEN WHATEVER WAS PUT IN
FRONT OF HIM WITH DECIDED INDIFFERENCE GREW INTO
A MAN WHO LIGHTS UP A KITCHEN. I STILL REALLY DON'T
GET HOW AND WHEN THIS TRANSFORMATION HAPPENED,
BUT THE MAN CAN COOK!

WHEN BEN COMES OVER TO MAKE US A MEAL (AND THANK-
FULLY THIS IS A FREQUENT EVENT), HE USUALLY RATTLES
OFF A MENU INVOLVING CUISINE FROM AT LEAST
THREE CONTINENTS. AS HE SETTLES INTO THE KITCHEN,
THERE IS A SENSE OF ANTICIPATION AND ALSO A HOLIDAY
FEELING. WHATEVER HE PLANS FOR US TO EAT, WE KNOW IT IS
GOING TO BE GOOD. HE USUALLY ARRIVES WITH A BAG OF INGRE-
DIENTS, KNOWING I MAY NOT HAVE THE CACTUS MOLD HE
NEEDS FOR HIS FISH TACOS OR HIS FAVORITE GARAM MASALA
FOR HIS INDIAN FOOD.

AS HE GETS ORGANIZED, THERE ARE APPETIZERS OFFERED
AND CONVERSATION TO BE SAVORED. IT IS HARD TO TELL WHAT
IF ANYTHING BEN IS ACTUALLY DOING BECAUSE THE FOCUS APPEARS
TO BE ON THE FUN, NOT THE PRODUCTION OF A MEAL. IN EARLY
YEARS OF HIS COOKING, THIS MADE ME NERVOUS. I WONDERED
IF HE NEEDED POINTERS. HOW COULD HE PAUSE TO TELL
SO MANY ANECDOTES, MOVE ABOUT THE KITCHEN IN SUCH A

RELAXED WAY AND GET A MEAL ON THE TABLE?

THESE CONCERNS OFTEN MANIFESTED IN WHAT MY CHILDREN CALL MY "BACKSEAT COOKING" OR WHAT I PREFER TO THINK OF AS THE OFFERING OF HELPFUL HINTS. SOON I LEARNED THAT THE BEST THING FOR ME TO DO WHEN BEN COOKS IS TO SIT BACK AND ENJOY THE MOMENT. WITH BEN AT THE HELM, A FABULOUS MEAL ALWAYS GETS TO THE TABLE WITH SURPRISING EFFICIENCY. HIS TECHNIQUE FAR SURPASSES MINE, AND HE NEEDS NO ADVICE. ONE MIGHT SAY THAT BEN REMEMBERS THINGS ESCOFFIER SAID, WHEREAS I VAGUELY REMEMBER WHO ESCOFFIER WAS.

BEN'S PROJECTS ARE AMBITIOUS. HE MAKES HIS OWN WINE. HIS FREEZER IS FULL OF THINGS LIKE HOPS FOR HOMEMADE BEER. BEN ALSO FORAGES FOR INGREDIENTS. WILD LEEK EXPEDITIONS ARE A NEAR DAILY OCCURRENCE IN EARLY SPRING. MORELS ARE ANOTHER ITEM SOUGHT AND FOUND.

SOUPS ARE A PARTICULAR SPECIALTY OF HIS, AND HE AQUIRED HIS REPETOIRE BY MAKING ALL OF JULIA CHILD'S SOUP RECIPES. SOMETIMES HIS MEALS REST ON A BEAUTIFUL BOWL OF SOUP PAIRED WITH A HOMEMADE BREAD, BUT USUALLY BEN IS ALL IN FROM SOUP TO NUTS. IF IT IS AN INDIAN MEAL ON THE DOCKET, HE MAKES SAMOSAS, HOMEMADE NAAN, BASMATI RICE, DAL, A CURRY OR TWO AND AN APPROPRIATE DRINK, OFTEN FROM SOME LIQUID HE HAS BEEN MARINATING WITH TWIGS AND BERRIES FOR A YEAR OR TWO.

DURING THE SCHOOL YEAR, BEN TEACHES HISTORY AND IS HEAD OF A DORMITORY OF FIFTY-FIVE TEENAGE BOYS. BEN TREATS ALL HIS CHARGES TO PANCAKE BREAKFASTS WITH OUR MAPLE SYRUP. HIS STUDENTS ALSO GIVE HIM FOOD OFFERINGS FROM THEIR HOMETOWNS FOR HIM TO COOK UP. IT IS NOT

UNCOMMON TO DROP IN ON BEN ON THE WEEKENDS AND FIND HIM GRILLING UP MOOSE DOGS OR ELK HAMBURGERS FOR HIS BOYS FROM ALASKA.

BEN BOUGHT TEDDY AND MALCOLM'S FARM. HE HAS A TENANT LIVING IN THE HOUSE RIGHT NOW, BUT HE WORKS THE LAND EACH SUMMER: STONEWALL BUILDING, CLEARING BRUSH, MANAGING HIS ORCHARD, WOODLOT AND HAY FIELDS, AND BUILDING OUTBUILDINGS. IN A FEW YEARS, HE WILL BE ABLE TO LIVE AT HIS FARM FULL TIME. WE THINK TEDDY WOULD BE SO VERY HAPPY TO HAVE BEN COOKING UP A STORM IN HER KITCHEN, RIGHT WHERE SHE COOKED SO MANY WONDERS HERSELF.

WHEN BEN MOVES NEXT DOOR, WE WILL SAVOR THE SHORT AND BEAUTIFUL COMMUTE TO OUR FAVORITE RESTAURANT. JUST DOWN THROUGH THE APPLE AND PEAR TREES AND PAST THE BLUEBERRIES WILL BE TEDDY'S KITCHEN RETURNED TO VIBRANT NEW LIFE AS CHEZ BEN. I HAVE MY RESERVATIONS IN ALREADY.

APPETIZERS

BAKED brie WITH CRANberrY Chutney

WE MAKE THIS DURING THE HOLIDAY SEASON AS iT iS Pretty AS Well AS WELL RECEIVED AT PARTIES. THERE ARE WILD CRANberrIES IN NEW HAMPSHIRE, WE ARE LUCKY ENOUGH TO KNOW A WOMEN WHO SElls HER HARVEST. SHE brAVEly COllECTS HER CRANberrIES FROM HER KAYAK ON COLD FALL DAYS.

TO MAKE CRANberrY ChutNEY:
- 2/3 CUP WATER
- 2/3 CUP SUGAR
- 1 1/3 CUP CRANberrIES
- 4 tsp CIDER VINEGAR
- 1/3 CUP DARK RAISINS
- 1/4 CUP CHOPPED WALNUTS
- 2 tsp. LIGHT brown SUGAR
- 1/4 tsp. GROUND GINGER
- 1/2 tsp CHOPPED GARLIC

COMbiNE WATER AND SUGAR IN HEAVY SAUCEPAN. STIR TO DISSOLVE THEN bring to boil WITHOUT STIRRING. ADD ALL THE OTHER INGREDIENTS. BOil VERY SLOWly StirriNG OCCASIONAlly UNTIL FAIRly THICK ABOUT 5 MINUTES. ChutNEY Will KEEP WELL iN REFRIGERATOR.

FOR BRIE AND CHUTNEY:
PLACE 2.2 lb WHEEL OF BRIE
ON PARCHMENT PAPER OR
FOIL ON A BAKING SHEET. SPREAD
CRANBERRY CHUTNEY OVER TOP.

REFRIGERATE 30 MINUTES
BEFORE BAKING. WHEN READY,
BAKE AT 350 DEGREES ON
MIDDLE SHELF OF OVEN FOR
8-10 MINUTES. SERVE WARM
WITH CRACKERS.

CAPONATA

THIS CAN BE SCOOPED UP WITH CRACKERS OR TOASTED FRENCH BREAD EVEN TOSSED ON PASTA. WE MAKE IT LATE IN THE SUMMER WHEN THE TOMATOES, EGGPLANTS AND PEPPERS ARE RIPE.

: 1 ½ lb. UNPEELED EGGPLANT CUT IN ¾ INCH DICE : ½ CUP ♡OLIVE OIL : 1 CUP COARSELY CHOPPED ONIONS : 3 OR 4 MEDIUM SWEET RED PEPPERS CUT IN ¾ INCH SQUARES : 1 CUP COARSELY CHOPPED CELERY : 8 Italian TYPE PASTE TOMATOES, PUREED IN BLENDER OR FOOD PROCESSOR TO MAKE TWO CUPS PUREE : ¼ CUP RED WINE VINEGAR : 2 Tbs. SUGAR : 1 Tbs. MINCED GARLIC : ½ CUP PITTED, SLICED OIL CURED BLACK ♡OLIVES : ¼ CUP CAPERS : SALT AND PEPPER :

PREHEAT OVEN TO 375. IN OIL, SAUTE ONIONS, PEPPERS AND CELERY IN AN OVEN PROOF DUTCH OVEN OR CAST IRON SKILLET FOR ABOUT FIVE MINUTES ON MEDIUM HIGH HEAT. ADD EGGPLANT AND SAUTE FOR FIVE MORE MINUTES. ADD TOMATO PUREE, VINEGAR, GARLIC, SUGAR AND SALT AND COOK A FEW MINUTES. BAKE CAPONATA FOR 20 MINUTES THEN ADD ♡OLIVES AND CAPERS. COOK FOR AT LEAST 15 MINUTES MORE UNTIL MOST OF THE LIQUID HAS EVAPORATED. COOL, SEASON WITH SALT AND PEPPER AND REFRIGERATE FOR A DAY TO MELD FLAVORS.

chicken WINGS

It's impossible to count how many different GREEN HOPE FARM SPORTING EVENTS have INVOLVED A PLATTER OF THESE BABIES!!

3 lbs. CHICKEN WINGS, DEJOINTED

MARINATE OVERNIGHT IN:

1/3 CUP SOY SAUCE

2 Tbs HONEY

2 Tbs CIDER VINEGAR

1 Tbs SESAME OIL

2 CLOVES GARLIC CRUSHED

1/4 tsp. CAYENNE

1 tsp. MINCED FRESH GINGER ROOT.

PREHEAT OVEN to 425°. ON RACK IN BAKING PANS PUT MARINATED CHICKEN WINGS. SPRINKLE WITH SESAME SEEDS. BAKE 30 MINUTES. IF NECESSARY TO REHEAT DO SO AT 350° FOR TEN MINUTES.

CRAB RANGOON

THIS IS ONE OF BEN'S RECIPES WHICH HE TOSSES TOGETHER AT LIGHTNING SPEED. THERE ARE NEVER ANY LEFT!

EIGHT OUNCES CRABMEAT
EIGHT OUNCES CREAM CHEESE
THREE SCALLIONS, SLICED.
ONE tsp. WORCESTERSHIRE SAUCE.
ONE tsp SOY SAUCE.
1/4 tsp. SALT, ONE tsp. SESAME OIL
ONE PACKAGE WONTON WRAPPERS
OIL FOR FRYING, PREFERABLY PEANUT.

MIX CRAB MEAT, CREAM CHEESE, SCALLIONS, WORCESTERSHIRE SAUCE, SOY SAUCE SESAME OIL AND SALT UNTIL IT COMBINES WELL.

IN THE MIDDLE OF EACH WONTON WRAPPER, PLACE A HEAPING PILE (TEASPOON) OF THE MIXTURE. WET THE EDGES AND FOLD IN HALF TO MAKE A TRIANGLE. (WET EDGES WITH WATER). SQUEEZE AIR OUT OF THE PACKET AND MAKE SURE ALL SEAMS ARE SEALED. WET ONE OF THE POINTED CORNERS THEN CONNECT THE TWO CORNERS, THE WET END FOLDED OVER THE OTHER TO CREATE A LITTLE CROWN OF HEAVEN. FRY IN OIL UNTIL GOLDEN BROWN AT 350 DEGREES. DO IN BATCHES TO MAINTAIN OIL TEMPERATURE AND DRAIN ON PAPER SUCH AS PAPER BAG BEFORE SERVING. DUCK SAUCE IS A GOOD CONDIMENT FOR THESE AS IS SWEET CHILI SAUCE.

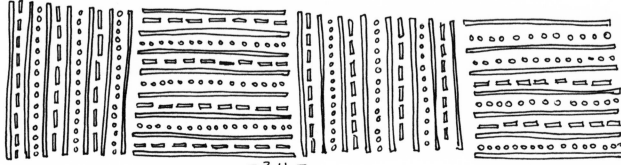

LAURA's
easiest

BEST BEAN DIP **EVER**.

LAURA CAME TO the farm FROM MINNESOTA, bearing MANY GREAT RECIPES. HERE is HER bean DiP, taste tested by LEGIONS OF TWENTY SOMETHINGS.

TWO CANS black beans
HALF JAR OF CHUNKY SALSA
MILD, MEDIUM OR HOT
LAURA SAYS "Choose YOUR ADVENTURE"
GROUND CUMIN to tASTE
Chili POWDER TO TASTE
LIME JUICE OF ONE LIME
CHEDDAR CHEESE, GRATED
TWO Tbs. CHOPPE CILANTRO

PREHEAT OVEN TO 350 DEGREES.

PUT BEANS IN A BAKING DISH. ADD SOME CUMIN, CHILI POWDER AND LIME JUICE AND THE SALSA. MIX TOGETHER AND GRATE ENOUGH CHEESE TO COVER — THE MORE CHEESE THE BETTER. BAKE UNCOVERED FOR ABOUT 45 MINUTES

SPRINKLE WITH FRESH CILANTRO AND SERVE WITH TACO Chips. LAURA'S NOTE: " THE bEAN DIP IS <u>HOT</u>! MAKE SURE YOU LET the BEAN DIP COOL DOWN A bit BEFORE YOU BRING IT OUT FOR FOLKS TO EAT. IT IS SO TASTY THAT IN THEIR EAGERNESS TO CONSUME, MANY PEOPLE HAVE BURNED THEIR MOUTHS ON THIS HOT BEANY GOODNESS!"

MIGUEL'S Salsa RECIPE

LIZZY'S HUSBAND, MIGUEL, WAS BORN AND RAISED IN SAN ANTONIO, TEXAS. HE HAS BEEN KEEPING US IN AMAZING TexMex FOOD SINCE HE FIRST MOVED HERE! WE LOVE his SALSA! HERE IS WHAT HE HAS TO SAY ABOUT IT, "ONE OF MY FIRST MEMORIES IS OF MY MOM MAKING SALSA. IN TEXAS, SALSA IS AN EVERY MEAL AFFAIR. IF YOU ARE NOT ADDING SALSA TO SOMETHING, IT'S A MYSTERY TO EVERYONE AROUND YOU. SALSA IS A REMINDER OF HOME, OF SIMPLE FLAVORS AND INGREDIENTS FRAGRANT AND TASTY."

ONE HANDFUL OR 25-30 STALKS OF CILANTRO. CHOPPED FINE INCLUDING STEMS • 1/2 ONION, DICED. • ONE FINGER SIZED CHILI PEPPER, DE-SEEDED AND CHOPPED • ONE tsp GROUND PEPPER • TWO tsp. SALT • JUICE OF 1/2 LEMON • 3-4 TOMATOES, DICED •

PLACE EVERYTHING but the LEMON JUICE IN A POT AT MEDIUM HEAT. BREW this FOR ABOUT FIVE MINUTES UNTil hot AND STEAMING but NOT boiling. While the SALSA IS BREWING, STAMP THE SALSA WITH A WOODEN SPOON OR MALLET. THIS WILL CAUSE the SALSA TO BE LIQUIDY. IF YOU WANT A CHUNKIER SALSA, DON'T STAMP the SALSA. ONCE the SALSA IS BREWED, SQUEEZE HALF A LEMON INTO THE POT AND ADD ADDITIONAL SALT AND PEPPER TO TASTE. LET SALSA COOL 15 MINUTES AND SERVE!

..... PiMENTO CHEESE.....

JIM GOES TO THE MASTERS GOLF TOURNAMENT
EACH SPRING IN A WELL-DESERVED BREAK FROM
TEACHING SIXTH GRADE AND   CHORES AT THE
FARM.

FOR MANY YEARS, JIM TALKED ABOUT THE PIMENTO CHEESE
SANDWICHES AVAILABLE ON THE COURSE. I KNOW THIS VERSION
IS PROBABLY NOT AUTHENTIC, but It SEEMS TO DO THE TRICK
BETWEEN TOURNAMENTS.... AT LEAST FOR JIM AND THE REST
OF US NEW ENGLANDERS.

I EXPECT TO HEAR FROM A LOT OF SOUTHERN
GREEN HOPE FARM FRIENDS ABOUT WHY THIS
IS REALLY NOT PIMENTO CHEESE! PLEASE SEND
RECIPES ALONG WITH YOUR COMMENTS!

1/2 lb EXTRA SHARP VERMONT CHEDDAR
1/2 CUP EXTRA SHARP NY CHEDDAR, ORANGE
ONE 7oz JAR PIMENTOS, DRAINED AND FINELY CHOPPED
1/2 tsp PEPPER
   CAYENNE TO TASTE
2/3 CUP MAYONNAISE

PUT ALL   INGREDIENTS
IN A FOOD PROCESSOR
   AND BLEND UNTIL WELL
MIXED bUT NOT
   COMPLETELY
      SMOOTH.

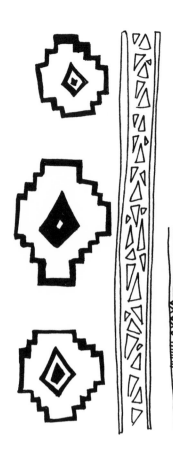

ROASTED TOMATILLO *Salsa*

before catherine boorady came to work at the farm, she lived in santa fe, new mexico. this is one of her recipes from her years there.

- ONE and A half lbs tomatillos, deHUSKED AND SOAKED IN Water UNTIL the stickiness IS GONE.

- ONE SERRANO OR TWO jalapeno chilis
  - THREE GARLIC CLOVES.
  - half cup CHOPPED FRESH CILANTRO
  - ONE LARGE ONION, COARSELY CHOPPED
  - TWO tsp. KOSHER SALT.

take SOAKED tomatillos, chiles garlic and BROIL ONE-TWO INCHES FROM heat, TURNING ONCE UNTIL tomatillos are softened AND slightly charred. PEEL GARLIC. PUT EVERYTHING IN A BLENDER AND BLENDERIZE.

TAPENADE

While oil cured olives are nicer, this is almost as good with canned black ♥olives.

◇ ½ lb. black♥olives, ◇ pitted and preferably oil cured.

◇ 3 Tbs. Capers ◇

◇ ½ cup basil leaves ◇

◇ 5 garlic cloves, peeled ◇

◇ Juice from 2 lemons ◇

◇ ⅔ cup olive oil. ◇

Process everything in a food processor until smooth then serve with toasted slices of French bread.

Optional: You can make this with anchovy filets (6)

SAMOSAS

THIS WONDERFUL RECIPE CAME FROM NEIGHBOR LESLIE MAC-GREGOR. WHEN I ASKED HER IF WE COULD SHARE HER RECIPE SHE SAID "PLEASE DO USE THE SAMOSA RECIPE. IT'S ALL ABOUT SPREADING THE MINISTRY OF SHARING SOUL FOOD, ISN'T IT?" MAKES ONE DOZEN.

DOUGH

TWO CUPS ALL PURPOSE FLOUR
HALF CUP CORN OIL
HALF CUP WATER.

IN FLAT PAN, MIX FLOUR AND OIL TOGETHER. KEEP MIXING WITH HANDS UNTIL ALL OIL IS ABSORBED INTO THE FLOUR. THEN ADD THE WATER SLOWLY. TRY TO CREATE A SMOOTH DOUGH. LET REST 10 MINUTES THEN DIVIDE INTO 6 BALLS AND PUT ASIDE.

MASALA

FOR THE FILLING, HEAT SKILLET THEN ADD OIL. WHEN OIL IS HOT, ADD CORIANDER, FENNEL AND POME-GRANATE SEEDS. STIR 30-60 SECONDS. ADD GINGER AND STIR FOR A MINUTE ADD FROZEN PEAS. COOK FOR 1-2 MINUTES. ADD POTATOES AND REST OF DRY SPICES. TURN OFF HEAT. MIX MASALA CAREFULLY AND ADD CHOPPED CILANTRO. DIVIDE INTO 12 PORTIONS.

MASALA

THREE LARGE POTATOES, BOILED, PEELED AND CHOPPED SMALL

ONE CUP FROZEN PEAS.
ONE TBS. WHOLE CORIANDER
ONE TBS WHOLE FENNEL.
ONE TSP WHOLE POMEGRAN-ATE SEEDS (THESE CAN BE PURCHASED DRY)

ONE TSP GROUND CAYENNE

ONE INCH PIECE GINGER ROOT, CHOPPED.

ONE TSP. SALT.

1/4 CUP CHOPPED CILANTRO
3 TBS. OIL.

ONE QUART OIL FOR FRYING.

ON A CLEAN SURFACE, ROLL DOUGH BALLS INTO 8-10" OBLONG DISKS. CUT IN HALF CROSSWISE. MOISTEN THE STRAIGHT EDGE WITH A LITTLE WATER, THEN CURL INTO A CONE SHAPE. TAKE ONE PORTION OF MASALA AND PUT INSIDE CONE. MAKE SURE YOU LEAVE 1/4" OF TOP EMPTY. MOISTEN ONE SIDE OF TOP EDGE WITH WATER AND THEN SEAL TO FORM A TRIANGLE. STAND EACH SAMOSA ON ITS SEALED EDGE. PREPARE ALL 12 SAMOSAS. HEAT OIL IN WOK OR DUTCH OVEN. WHEN OIL IS HOT FOR DEEP FRYING, FRY FOUR SAMOSAS AT A TIME ON HIGH HEAT, 5-6 MINUTES UNTIL GOLDEN BROWN. REMOVE FROM OIL. SERVE WITH DHANIA AND IMLI CHUTNEY. RECIPES FOLLOW FOR BOTH THESE CHUTNEYS.

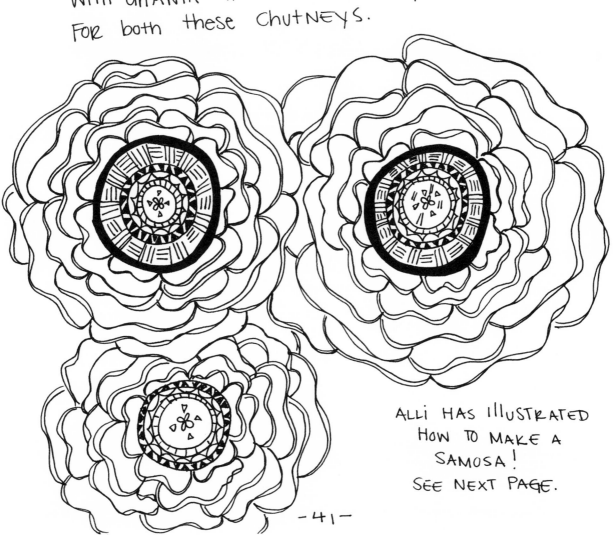

ALLI HAS ILLUSTRATED HOW TO MAKE A SAMOSA! SEE NEXT PAGE.

SAMOSA ~
CONSTRUCTION

 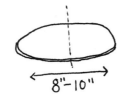 CUT IN HALF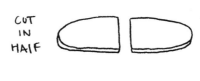

8"-10"

FOLD UP CORNERS

PUT IN *filling*

FOLD UP ENDS TO MAKE

ENJOY!

TWO Chutneys
FOR SAMOSAs

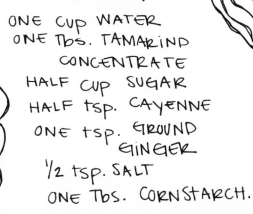

IMLI TAMARIND CHUTNEY

ONE CUP WATER
ONE Tbs. TAMARIND CONCENTRATE
HALF CUP SUGAR
HALF tsp. CAYENNE
ONE tsp. GROUND GINGER
1/2 tsp. SALT
ONE Tbs. CORNSTARCH.

MIX ALL INGREDIENTS TOGETHER AND PUT IN A SAUCEPAN. BRING TO BOIL AND ALLOW SAUCE TO THICKEN. TURN DOWN HEAT TO SIMMER ONE MORE MINUTE. THIS WILL THICKEN MORE AFTER IT IS COOLED DOWN.

DHANIA CILANTRO CHUTNEY

CAN KEEP FOR 4-6 MONTHS IN THE REFRIGERATOR but IT WON'T STAY THE SAME VIBRANT GREEN.

ONE CUP CHOPPED CILANTRO, 5 CLOVES CHOPPED GARLIC, TWO Tbs. LEMON JUICE ONE Tbs. WHOLE CUMIN, ONE INCH PIECE OF GINGER, CHOPPED, ONE tsp SALT, 3 GREEN CHILIS OR 1 LARGE JALAPENO, SCANT 1/2 CUP WATER.

ADD INGREDIENTS TO A BLENDER AND PUREE.

MYSTERY DIP

THIS ONE IS FOR CHARLIE...
AND MAYBE LAUREN TOO!

THIS SUMMER WE built A NEW BARN THAT WE NAMED ROCK RILEY. TO CELEBRATE ROCK RILEY'S COMPLETION, WE HAD A BIG PARTY. STAFF GODDESS, LAURA, PLAYED WITH HER BAND, AND WE DANCED THE NIGHT AWAY.

AT A POORLY lit FOOD TABLE, VEGETARIAN STAFFER LAUREN SETTLED IN TO CHOW DOWN ON THIS DIP. NEXT MORNING, SHE discovered SHE'd been FEASTING ON CHIPPED BEEF! I MADE THE DIP FOR EMILY'S boyFRIEND CHARLIE WHO IS A BIG FAN OF CHiPPED BEEF, but APPARENTLY IT WAS IRRESISTIble EVEN TO VEGETARIANS.

½ CUP CHIPPED BEEF, FINEly CHOPPED • 8 oz PACKAGE OF CREAM CHEESE • (CREAM CHEESE SHOULD bE SOFTENED.) • 1 CUP SOUR CREAM • 2 Tbs. DRIED MINCED ONION • 1 green PEPPER • (PEPPER SHOULD bE FINEly CHOPPED) • ½ CUP CHOPPED PECANS • SALT AND PEPPER TO TASTE. •

LAUREN LIKED this WITH POTATO CHIPS. SO DID EVERY ONE ELSE.

breakfast and bread

ALMOND
POPPY SEED
MUFFINS

OUR FRIEND EMILY CROMWELL FIDDLED WITH THIS RECIPE UNTIL SHE GOT IT JUST RIGHT BEFORE BEGINNING A SHORT BUT BRILLIANT CAREER IN THE MUFFIN BUSINESS AT OUR LOCAL FARMER'S MARKET. WE APPRECIATED THAT SHE WAS SO WILLING TO SHARE HER RECIPE WHEN SHE RETIRED FROM MUFFIN CREATION.

1/2 CUP BUTTER, 2 CUPS SUGAR, 2 EGGS, 1 CUP YOGURT, 2 Tbs ALMOND EXTRACT, 2 CUPS FLOUR, AT LEAST 1/4 CUP POPPY SEEDS, 1/2 tsp SALT, 1/4 tsp BAKING SODA

CREAM BUTTER AND ONE CUP OF THE SUGAR. BEAT IN EGGS ONE AT A TIME THEN STIR IN YOGURT AND ALMOND EXTRACT. IN SEPARATE BOWL COMBINE FLOUR, POPPY SEEDS, REMAINING SUGAR AND BAKING SODA. ADD TO CREAMED MIXTURE AND BLEND UNTIL JUST MOISTENED. POUR INTO GREASED MUFFIN TINS OR CUP CAKE PAPERS AND SPRINKLE WITH SLICED ALMONDS. BAKE AT 400° FOR 15-20 MINUTES

APPLE bUTTER
Streusel Coffee Cake

When it is a good apple year, we make lots of applesauce and apple butter (which is really just applesauce cooked down further). Here is one of our breakfast recipes using apple butter.

HALF CUP MELTED bUTTER
1½ CUP FLOUR
3/4 CUP bROWN SUGAR
1 tsp. bAKING SODA
1tsp. CINNAMON
1 tsp. VANILLA
ONE CUP APPLE bUTTER
ONE EGG

MIX TOGETHER AND POUR INTO 9x9" GREASED PAN. MIX AND SPRINKLE ON TOP OF BATTER: 1/4 CUP SUGAR, 1/4 CUP bROWN SUGAR, 1/4 FLOUR, 1/4 tsp. CINNAMON, 1/4 tsp NUTMEG, 1/4 CUP butter, 1/2 CUP NUTS.

SOMETIMES I DOUbIE THIS TOPPING. WhATEVER, bAKE AT 350° FOR 40 MINUTES. TRY NOT TO COOK this UNTIL IT IS DRy. IT IS better MOIST.

APPLE WALNUT MUFFINS:

AN APPLE MUFFIN WITH A NICE CINNAMON NUT SPRINKLE ON TOP.

1½ CUP SMALL APPLE CHUNKS

1¾ CUP FLOUR

2 tsp. BAKING POWDER

2 tsp GROUND CINNAMON (SAVE 1 tsp. OUT FOR TOPPING)

⅔ CUP BROWN SUGAR, PACKED.

½ CUP HONEY

¼ CUP PLAIN YOGURT

½ SAFFLOWER OR OTHER FLAVORLESS OIL

1 tsp VANILLA

2 EGGS

½ CUP CHOPPED WALNUTS

HEAPING Tbs. BROWN SUGAR FOR THE TOP.

MIX BROWN SUGAR, HONEY, YOGURT, EGGS, VANILLA TOGETHER. GENTLY MIX DRY INGREDIENTS INTO THIS WET MIXTURE THEN ADD ALL THE APPLES PIECES AND HALF THE NUTS. DON'T OVER MIX!

PUT BATTER INTO PAPER MUFFIN CUPS IN MUFFIN TINS. TAKE THE OTHER HALF OF THE NUTS, ADD THE OTHER tsp. OF CINNAMON AND THE HEAPING Tbs. OF BROWN SUGAR THEN SPRINKLE ON TOP OF MUFFINS. BAKE 15-20 MINUTES.

IN PRE HEATED 375° OVEN. LET THEM SET A FEW MINUTES BEFORE TAKING THEM OUT OF THE MUFFIN TINS!

— ben's famous —

PORTER ALE BREAD

BEN FOUND THIS QUICK BREAD RECIPE
DURING HIS SENIOR YEAR IN COLLEGE
AND STILL MAKES IT FREQUENTLY
FOR ONE AND ALL. IT HAS WONDERFUL
CRUST.

- THREE TBS. MELTED
    BUTTER
- THREE CUPS UNBLEACHED
    WHITE FLOUR
- ONE TBS. BAKING
    POWDER
- TWO TBS + ONE TSP. SUGAR
- ONE TSP. SALT
- ONE AND A HALF CUPS
    DARK BEER. (PORTER ALE IS GOOD!!)

PREHEAT OVEN TO THREE HUNDRED AND SEVENTY-
FIVE DEGREES. BRUSH A STANDARD LOAF PAN WITH
HALF THE MELTED BUTTER. PUT ALL DRY INGREDIENTS
TOGETHER IN A BOWL AND MIX. ADD BEER AND
MIX QUICKLY, FOLDING BEER INTO DRY
INGREDIENTS. DRIZZLE REMAINING
BUTTER ON TOP OF DOUGH. BAKE
FOR FORTY FIVE TO FIFTY
MINUTES. UNTIL GOLDEN
BROWN. SERVE WARM.

BEN'S
NAAN

ONE Tbs. YEAST
ONE CUP LUKEWARM WATER
FOUR Tbs. SUGAR OR
  HONEY OR MAPLE SYRUP.
ONE BEATEN EGG
  TWO tsp. SALT
THREE Tbs. MILK
ABOUT FOUR CUPS FLOUR.

WHEN WE HAVE INDIAN FOOD, SOMEONE IS ALMOST ALWAYS HAPPY TO THROW TOGETHER A BATCH OR TWO OF NAAN. WE CREDIT BEN WITH THE RECIPE AND IT IS USUALLY HIM COOKING UP THE NAAN.

PROOF YEAST, WATER AND SUGAR TOGETHER FOR A FEW MINUTES THEN ADD BEATEN EGG AND MILK. SLOWLY ADD FLOUR UNTIL THE DOUGH HAS A SOFT CONSISTENCY BUT IS NOT TOO STICKY TO KNEAD BRIEFLY. LET DOUGH RISE UNDER A DISHCLOTH IN A WARM PLACE FOR AN HOUR OR SO.

CUT DOUGH INTO GOLF BALL SIZED PIECES THEN PULL AND FLATTEN EACH INTO FOUR INCH DISCS. WE COOK THE NAAN IN AN ELECTRIC FRY PAN THAT IS SLIGHTLY OILED. A TEMPERATURE 350° OR HOTTER WORKS WELL. IN A COUPLE MINUTES YOU WILL NEED TO FLIP OVER THE BREAD TO COOK ON THE OTHER SIDE. THIS MAKES ABOUT A DOZEN NAAN, AND IF YOUR HOUSEHOLD IS ANYTHING LIKE OURS, THERE WON'T BE ANY LEFTOVER.

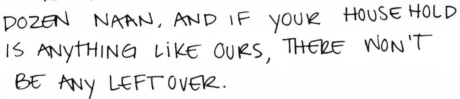

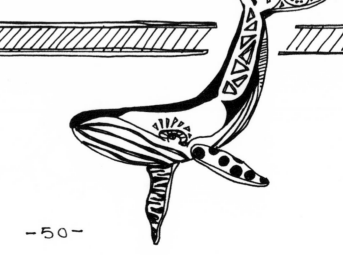

BLUEBERRY MUFFINS with the ZING OF Lemon

these are a bit different than the usual cinnamon flavored blueberry muffin. oddly enough, frozen blueberries work particularly well with this recipe so we make these after the harvest.

- 3¼ cups flour
- ½ tsp. salt
- 1½ cup sugar
- 4 tsp. baking powder
- 1 tsp. baking soda
- 1 Tbs. grated lemon rind
- 2 eggs
- 2 cups buttermilk
- ½ vegetable oil
- 1 or more cups blueberries (I use more)

sift dry ingredients together with lemon rind. in a separate bowl, whisk eggs, buttermilk and oil until well mixed. add this to the dry ingredients and stir until just mixed. gently fold in blueberries. spoon batter into muffin cups lined with muffin papers. fill to brim. you will probably get about 16 muffins. bake at 375° for 20 minutes. cool for 10 minutes before removing from the muffin tins.

buttermilk
Pancakes.

ben frequently does pancake breakfasts for his high school students and this is the pancake recipe he uses. They really ARE Superior pancakes as ARE ALL his students!

- TWO EGGS
- ONE AND A HALF CUPS buttermilk
- ONE CUP MILK
- TWO CUPS FLOUR
- ONE tsp SALT
- TWO Tbs SUGAR
- 1/4 tsp baking SODA
- ONE Tbs baking POWDER
- THREE Tbs OIL or MELTED butter

Whisk eggs, buttermilk AND MILK together. ADD the REST of the IN-gredients AND Whisk all together. DON't worry ABOUT LUMPS.

IN LAURA'S FAMILY THIS
CORNBREAD IS EATEN
WITH SPICY CHILI.

Carpenter
FAMILY
CORNBREAD!

PREHEAT OVEN TO
350° THEN TURN OVEN
TO 300° WHEN CORN-
BREAD GOES IN THE
OVEN.

½ lb butter (two sticks)
1 cup SUGAR or (¾ cup HONEY)
4 EGGS
1 CAN CHOPPED GREEN CHILIS
1½ CUP FROZEN OR FRESH CORN.
½ CUP MILK
1 CUP GRATED CHEDDAR
½ tsp SALT
1 CUP FLOUR
1 CUP CORN MEAL
4 tsp. BAKING POWDER
PINCH BAKING SODA

CREAM BUTTER AND SUGAR, ADD EGGS THEN ADD
REST OF INGREDIENTS. MIX THOROUGHLY AND POUR
INTO A 9X13 INCH GREASED BAKING PAN. BAKE FOR
ABOUT AN HOUR.

Challah

A CELEBRATORY BREAD MADE FAMOUS IN OUR CLAN by EMILY who MAKES It FOR ALL OCCASIONS, big AND SMALL.

2-4 tsp. YEAST

2 to 2½ CUPS bREAD FLOUR

¾ tsp. SALT

5 Tbs. SUGAR OR HONEY

1½ Tbs. dRY SKIM MILK POWDER

1½ Tbs. BUTTER

¾ CUP WATER (A little LESS IF USING HONEY)

1 lARGE EGG, BEATEN. (TO BRUSH ON BEFORE BAKING)

SEt WATER, SUGAR, SALT AND YEAST IN MIXING BOWL TO PROOF FOR A FEW MINUTES. ADD ALL OTHER INGREDIENTS AND KNEAD UNTIL SMOOTH AND SILKY. ADD A BIT MORE FLOUR IF NEEDED. LET RISE UNTIL DOUBLE IN SIZE, PUNCH DOWN SEPARATE INTO THREE STRANDS. BRAID the DOUGH AND SEAL UNDER ENDS. It IS TRADITIONAL to BLESS the BREAD AT THIS TIME. BRUSH WITH EGG AND LET SIT FOR AT LEAST 15 MINUTES UNTIL IT HAS BEGUN TO RISE AGAIN. BAKE AT 350° FOR 20 OR SO MINUTES OR UNTIL GOLDEN BROWN.

CORN
C·A·K·E·S

MY GRANDMOTHER HAD THESE EVERY MORNING FOR BREAKFAST DURING HER CHILDHOOD IN St. LOUIS MISSOURI. MY GRANDMOTHER, KITTY, AND HER YOUNGER SISTER LIZZIE GOT SO TIRED OF THEM THAT THEY WOULD THROW THEM OUT THE WINDOW.

THE ONLY PROBLEM WAS THAT THE CORN CAKES FELL IN THE WINDOW BOXES OF THE WOMAN WHO LIVED DOWNSTAIRS FROM THEM, AND THIS WOMAN REPORTED THE FLYING CORN CAKE'S TO MY GRANDMOTHER'S MOTHER.

GREAT!
MY GRANDMOTHER WAS A FRIEND OF IRMA ROMBAUER, THE CREATOR OF "THE JOY OF COOKING", but SHE HER-SELF WAS NOT A COOK... THE CORN CAKE INCIDENT WAS NOT REPORTED TO IRMA AS THERE WAS ALREADY QUITE ENOUGH HUMBLE PIE GOING AROUND SINCE EVERY ATTEMPT TO HAVE IRMA ROMBAUER TO DINNER BROUGHT ON AN EPIC KICHEN DISASTER.

ONE EGG, ONE CUP BUTTERMILK, 1/2 tsp BAKING SODA, 3/4 tsp SALT, 3/4 CUP CORN MEAL.

OUR LIZZY HAS MADE THESE A BREAKFAST STAPLE IN OUR HOUSE AND SO FAR, NONE HAVE GONE FLYING! MIX BATTER AND SERVE WITH MAPLE SYRUP.

CRANBERRY
ORANGE NUT
Bread

THIS IS FROM THE THANKS-
GIVING TABLE OF MY SISTER
IN LAW KATY SHEEHAN.

PREHEAT OVEN TO

350°

GREASE TWO BREAD
PANS.

3 CUPS COARSELY CHOPPED
CRANBERRIES

1 CUP CHOPPED NUTS

GRATED RIND OF
2 ORANGES

2 EGGS, BEATEN PLUS JUICE OF
TWO ORANGES PLUS MILK TO
MAKE TWO CUPS.

5 CUPS FLOUR

2 1/2 CUPS SUGAR

5 tsp BAKING POWDER

2 tsp SALT

2/3 CUP BUTTER

CREAM BUTTER WITH SUGAR AND THEN OTHER
DRY INGREDIENTS. ADD LIQUIDS THEN FOLD IN
FRUITS AND NUTS. POUR INTO GREASED PANS
AND BAKE FOR ONE HOUR AND TEN MINUTES

FANCY
PANCAKES

Lauren Lenz, PERENNIAL STAFF *goddess*, SHARED THIS RECIPE EXPLAINING, "DON'T LET THE TITLE FOOL YOU — though this delicious EGGY PANCAKE MAY APPEAR TO BE SOMETHING MORE COMPLICATED than your AVERAGE BREAKFAST, IT'S ACTUALLY THE BEST THING TO MAKE ON A LAZY SUNDAY. THROW IT TOGETHER, pop it IN THE OVEN FOR 45 MINUTES, AND SETTLE IN WITH A CUP OF TEA AND FAVORITE BOOK (OR HEAD BACK TO BED FOR A bit). WHEN IT COMES OUT IT WILL APPEAR LIKE YOU'VE PUT A LOT OF EFFORT INTO MAKING SOMETHING FANCY, AND ONLY YOU WILL KNOW HOW EASY IT WAS TO CREATE."

1½ CUP FLOUR 2¼ tsp BAKING POWDER
ONE tsp. SALT FOUR EGGS 1½ CUP MILK
¼ CUP OIL SEASONAL FRUIT OF YOUR
CHOICE (blueberries, blackberries, APPLES,
STRAWBERRIES ARE ALL GOOD.)

PREHEAT OVEN TO 350 DEGREES. COMBINE DRY INGREDIENTS. SEPARATE EGGS. COMBINE YOLKS WITH MILK AND OIL. COMBINE DRY AND WET INGREDIENTS. BEAT AND MIX IN EGG WHITES, FOLDING IN UNTIL JUST BARELY MIXED. HEAT 2 Tbs butter IN CAST-IRON FRYING PAN. ADD batter AND FRUIT OF CHOICE. BAKE 45 MINUTES OR UNTIL BROWNED ON TOP. SERVE WITH MAPLE SYRUP AND PLAIN YOGURT ON YOUR FANCIEST CHINA.

DARK WHEAT bread

JIM'S FATHER, MEL WAS THE REASON WE WERE ABLE TO BUILD OUR FARMHOUSE. HE TOLD US WE COULD BUILD A HOUSE THEN HELPED US EVERY STEP OF THE WAY. COMING UP FOR NUMEROUS WEEKENDS TO WIRE, PLUMB OR DEMONSTRATE TO JIM THE NEXT TASK ON JIM'S LIST OF SKILLS TO LEARN AND THINGS TO DO. MEL WAS EVER CHEERFUL PROVIDED THERE WAS SOUP AND THIS BREAD WAITING FOR HIM AT DAY'S END.

• 2 2/3 CUP STRONG COFFEE • 2/3 CUP WATER • 1/3 CUP HONEY • 1 Tbs. SALT • 1 PACKAGE DRY YEAST • 1/2 CUP WARM WATER • 1/2 CUP YELLOW CORNMEAL • 4 1/2 CUPS STONE GROUND WHOLE WHEAT FLOUR • 4 CUPS WHITE FLOUR •

ONE PACKAGE DRY YEAST = 2 1/4 tsp.

COMBINE COFFEE, 2/3 CUP OF WATER,
HONEY AND SALT. COOL TO LUKEWARM.
COMBINE YEAST AND 1/2 CUP OF WARM
WATER. LET STAND TO PROOF. ADD TO
COFFEE MIXTURE. STIR IN CORNMEAL
AND AS MUCH OF THE FLOUR AS POSSIBLE.
KNEAD IN THE REST. KNEAD UNTIL
SMOOTH ABOUT TEN MINUTES. PLACE
IN GREASED BOWL AND TURN DOUGH
TO GREASE TOP. COVER AND LET RISE
UNTIL DOUBLE IN BULK. PUNCH DOWN.
SHAPE INTO TWO LOAVES. PLACED IN
GREASED BREAD PANS. COVER AND LET
RISE UNTIL JUST BELOW TOPS OF PANS.
BAKE AT 375 FOR 45 MINUTES. REMOVE
FROM PANS AND COOL ON RACKS.

Dill Casserole Bread

ONE SUMMER DURING COLLEGE, I WORKED AS A WAIT-
RESS/CHAMBERMAID AT AN ISOLATED LODGE ON
A LAKE IN THE ADIRONDACKS. THE WOMAN WHO RAN THE
PLACE, AFFECTIONATELY KNOWN AS MA BOSS, WAS AN
INCREDIBLE COOK WHO DAILY WHIPPED UP HUGE
AMOUNTS OF SOUPS, STEWS, CAKES, PIES AND BREADS
TO FEED COUNTLESS FISHERMEN. THE ONLY WAY
TO GET TO THE LODGE WAS BY BOAT BUT THIS
DIDN'T SEEM TO SLOW ANYONE DOWN. FOLKS
CAME IN DROVES, AND WE WERE BOOKED FULL
EVERY NIGHT WITH SOGGY CAMPERS IN FOR
A HOT MEAL AS WELL AS THOSE FISHERMEN
ACTUALLY STAYING AT THE LODGE.

EACH NIGHT AFTER SERVICE THE OTHER WAITRESS
AND I WERE ALLOWED TO EAT ANY LEFTOVER PIE.
WE PARTICULARLY LIKED THE COCONUT CREAM PIE.
SO WHEN TELLING GUESTS ABOUT THE EVENING'S
PIE OPTIONS, WE WOULD OFTEN WAX POETIC ABOUT
THE AMAZING APPLE PIE AND BRILLIANT BLUE-
BERRY PIE... THEN SOFT PEDAL THE COCONUT
PIE AVAILABLE. IT WAS ALWAYS OUR HOPE THAT
GUESTS WOULDN'T EAT ALL THE COCONUT
CREAM PIE. BUT MA BOSS WAS A FAMOUS COOK
AND FAMOUS FOR THIS PIE IN PARTICULAR SO
MOST OF THE TIME THERE WAS NARY A
SLICE LEFT.

MA BOSS DIDN'T SHARE HER PIE RECIPES,
BUT I DID GET THIS RECIPE FROM HER.
SHE WOULD COOK IT IN CERAMIC BOWLS AND
SOME OF THOSE FISHERMEN WOULD EAT A WHOLE

ROUND LOAF ALL by THEMSELVES (AND THEN STill EAT THE COCONUT CREAM PIE TOO.)

ONE PACKAGE DRY YEAST (2 1/4 tsp)
1/4 CUP WATER
ONE CUP CREAMED COTTAGE CHEESE
TWO Tbs. SUGAR
ONE Tbs. butter
ONE Tbs. MINCED DRY ONION
TWO tsp. DRIED Dill SEED OR
    Dill WEED (YOU CAN ALSO
    USE FRESH, IN WHICH
    CASE USE MORE.)
ONE tsp. SALT
    1/4 tsp bAKING SODA
ONE UNBEATEN EGG
2 1/4 to 2 1/2 CUPS FLOUR
MELTED butter AND PARMESAN
        CHEESE.

SOFTEN YEAST IN WARM WATER. COMBINE IN bowl THE COTTAGE CHEESE, SUGAR, ONION, butter, Dill, SALT, SODA AND EGG. ADD THE SOFTENED YEAST. ADD ENOUGH FLOUR TO FORM A STIFF DOUGH. KNEAD UNTIL WELL MIXED. COVER AND LET RISE UNTIL DOUBLE IN bULK, USUAlly ABOUT AN HOUR bUT SOMETIMES FASTER IN THE RAIN FOREST THAT IS THE ADIRONDACK PARK. STIR DOWN DOUGH AND TURN INTO A WELL GREASED OVEN PROOF bowl. LET RISE ANOTHER HALF HOUR OR SO UNTIL LIGHT. BAKE AT 350° FOR 40-50 MINUTES OR UNTIL GOLDEN brown. BRUSH WITH MELTED butter AND SPRINKLE WITH CHEESE.

GINGER Scones

WHILE DEB CARDEN BROUGHT THIS RECIPE
TO OUR ATTENTION, LIZZY IS THE ONE WHO
HAS MADE THESE SCONES ABOUT TEN
THOUSAND TIMES FOR THE OFFICE STAFF.

TWO CUPS FLOUR
1/3 CUP SUGAR
ONE TBS BAKING POWDER
ONE tsp. GROUND GINGER
DASH OF SALT
ONE tsp. GRATED LEMON PEEL
12 Tbs. COLD BUTTER
3/4 CUP WHIPPING CREAM

2/3 CUP CRYSTALLIZED GINGER, CHOPPED
TWO tsp. WHIPPING CREAM
AND ADDITIONAL SUGAR FOR TOP.

PREHEAT OVEN TO
400°

MIX FLOUR, SUGAR, BAKING POWDER,
GINGERS, SALT AND LEMON ZEST. CUT
BUTTER IN PATS THEN MIX BY HAND
UNTIL MIXTURE RESEMBLES FINE
CRUMBS. MAKE HOLE IN CENTER AND
ADD CREAM. MIX UNTIL IT HOLDS
TOGETHER THEN KNEAD ON COUNTER
INTO SMOOTH BALL. CHILL.

AFTER CHILLING, MAKE BALL INTO
TWO 3/4" DISKS SIX INCH ACROSS.
WRAP AND FREEZE FOR 15 MINUTES.
WITH SHARP KNIFE CUT EACH DISK
INTO EIGHT WEDGES. BRUSH WITH
CREAM AND SPRINKLE WITH SUGAR.
BAKE UNTIL EDGES ARE JUST
BROWN, 15 MINUTES.

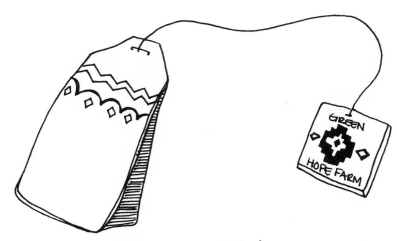

ENJOY WITH A
GREAT
CUP OF TEA♥

the granola.

after trying a lot of different recipes, we settled on this one.

- Six cups rolled oats -
- one cup wheat flakes -
- one cup rye flakes -
- one cup cashews or almonds -
- one cup sunflower seeds -
- half cup sesame seeds -
- half cup flour -
- one cup brown sugar -
- half cup oil -
- half cup honey -
- one tbs. vanilla. -

Mix sugar, oil, honey and vanilla then mix with dry ingredients.

Spread on cookie sheets then bake in three fifty degrees oven, turning frequently until

golden brown.

MAPLE MUFFINS WITH MAPLE glaze

THESE ARE OUR FAVORITE MUFFINS. The only trick is getting the muffins out of the tin in one PIECE A FEW MINUTES AFTER COOKING them. THIS has to be done so the GLAZE CAN GO INTO the bottom of the tin and the muffin can go back in to SOAK up the GLAZE. SO BUTTER YOUR MUFFIN TIN WELL!

TWO EGGS
ONE CUP YOGURT
ONE CUP MAPLE SYRUP
ONE CUP FLOUR
ONE tsp. SODA
THREE FORTHS CUP CHOPPED WALNUTS
ONE CUP BRAN FLAKES NOT the CEREAL but real bran flake

(I sometimes substitute wheat germ which works just as well.)

Makes a DOZEN MUFFINS!

beat eggs with a fork. stir in yogurt and syrup. ADD FLOUR, bran and SODA. stir UNTIL JUST MOISTENED. BAKE AT FOUR HUNDRED DEGREES FOR FIFTEEN — TWENTY MINUTES IN well buttered MUFFIN TINS. REMOVE FROM TINS While WARM. HEAT GLAZE. SPOON INTO the bottom OF MUFFIN TINS and PUT MUFFINS back INTO TINS. LET STAND FOR FIFTEEN MINUTES TO ABSORB GLAZE.

glaze

TWO THIRDS CUP Maple syrup.

SIX Tbs BUTTER.

-65-

RAISIN - PECAN BREAD

STARTER

This bread is so wonderful. It almost makes a meal! Begin this two days before you want to eat it. You can bake it at night to eat the following morning

1 Tbs. sugar
1 cup lukewarm water
1 Tbs. dry yeast.
2 cups all purpose flour

STEP ONE Combine the sugar and water in a bowl, sprinkle with yeast then stir. Gradually stir in the flour until the mixture is smooth. Transfer to a plastic container. Cover and refrigerate.

DOUGH

2 cups warm water
2 tsp. salt
3 cups organic raisins, soaked in 3 cups boiling water for 20 minutes then drained
2 cups pecans.
1/2 cup whole wheat flour
4-5 cups all purpose
 (King Arthur is good)
extra flour for kneading
corn meal for dusting

STEP TWO Put starter in bowl and slowly add water, whipping with a flat whip. It will be messy. Add salt, raisins and pecans.

STEP THREE

Beat in flours a few spoonful at a time. Stop adding flour when the mixture forms a very sticky dough; resist adding extra flour or bread will be dry. Continue to beat or knead for 5 minutes. Transfer dough to large oiled bowl or plastic container and refrigerate for 6-8 hours.

PUNCH DOWN THE DOUGH, DIVIDE IN HALF AND
SHAPE EACH PIECE INTO OVAL LOAVES WITH
TAPERED ENDS. DUST TOPS WITH FLOUR AND
DUST BAKING SHEET WITH CORN MEAL. SLASH
BREAD DIAGONALLY 4 TIMES ACROSS THE TOP
WITH SHARP KNIFE. TRANSFER TO SHEET
AND LET REST IN A WARM PLACE FOR 30
MINUTES.

SET THE OVEN FOR 400 DEGREES. IF YOU
HAVE A PIZZA STONE, PUT IT ON BOTTOM
SHELF AND LET IT HEAT FOR 20 MINUTES.
LIFT BREAD OFF BAKING SHEET AND
TRANSFER TO STONE. IF YOU DO NOT
HAVE A STONE, YOU CAN PUT IT RIGHT
IN THE OVEN ON THE BAKING SHEET.

NO MATTER HOW YOU DO IT, THIS BREAD
IS MOIST WITH AN INCREDIBLE TASTE.

BAKE FOR 45-50 MINUTES OR UNTIL
LOAVES SOUND HOLLOW WHEN TAPPED
ON THE BOTTOM.

ORANGE
PECAN
Scones

ELIZABETH IS OUR SCONE QUEEN
AND KEEPS THE OFFICE IN SCONES
OF ALL FLAVORS.

ZEST OF ONE ORANGE
1/2 CUP DRIED CURRANTS
3-4 Tbs. ORANGE JUICE
 (FRESH SQUEEZED)
THREE CUPS FLOUR
FIVE Tbs. SUGAR
ONE Tbs. BAKING POWDER
1/2 tsp. SALT
ONE STICK BUTTER
1/3 CUP MILK PLUS 1 Tbs.
ONE EGG YOLK BEATEN
1/4 CUP PECANS
 COARSELY CHOPPED.
1/3 CUP YOGURT

PREHEAT OVEN TO 400°. PLACE
CURRANTS AND ZEST IN BOWL
WITH ORANGE JUICE AND LET
SIT HALF HOUR TO ABSORB JUICE.
MIX TOGETHER 1/3 CUP MILK
AND YOGURT. MIX TOGETHER
EGG YOLK AND 1 Tbs. MILK. SIFT
TOGETHER DRY INGREDIENTS. CUT
BUTTER INTO DRY INGREDIENTS
USING A PASTRY CUTTER. MIXTURE
SHOULD RESEMBLE COARSE MEAL.
POUR MILK MIXTURE, CURRANTS
AND JUICE OVER DRY AND MIX
IN A FEW SWIFT STROKES. ADD
A BIT MORE MILK IF IT LOOKS
LIKE THE MIXTURE WON'T HOLD
TOGETHER. PAT INTO CIRCLE 10" ACROSS AND 1" THICK. PAINT
TOP WITH EGG YOLK AND PAT ON PECANS. CUT INTO EIGHT
WEDGES AND PLACE ON BAKING SHEET. BAKE
UNTIL BROWNED 20 MINUTES.

WAFFLES

This is our favorite waffle recipe, and of course, we think they are best served with REAL MAPLE SYRUP.

- FOUR EGGS
- TWO CUPS SIFTED FLOUR
- ONE tsp. SALT
- ONE tsp BAKING SODA
- ONE tsp. BAKING POWDER
- TWO CUPS BUTTERMILK
- HALF CUP MELTED BUTTER

Beat eggs until light. Sift flour, salt, baking soda, and baking powder. Add flour mixture and buttermilk alternately to eggs beginning and ending with flour mixture. Add melted butter and blend thoroughly.

YORKSHIRE
PUDDING

WHEN I WAS LITTLE, WE HAD THIS FOR SUNDAY LUNCH AND HOLIDAY MEALS ALWAYS WITH ROAST BEEF. ON ONE OCCASION, MY MOTHER HAD LEFT A BLENDER FULL OF THIS BATTER IN THE REFRIGERATOR, AND MY LITTLE BROTHER, MATTHEW, THOUGHT IT WAS A MILKSHAKE AND POURED HIMSELF A BIG GLASS OF THE STUFF. HE WAS SO HORRIFIED WHEN HE TASTED HIS MILKSHAKE THAT HE DROPPED HIS GLASS AND THE WHOLE BLENDER ON THE GROUND. IT WAS QUITE A MESS!

TWO CUPS SIFTED FLOUR: HALF tsp SALT: TWO CUPS WHOLE MILK OR HALF AND HALF: FOUR EGGS: EIGHT Tbs. BEEF DRIPPINGS OR BUTTER:

SIFT FLOUR AND SALT. PUT MILK IN A BLENDER. ADD FLOUR. BLENDERIZE THEN ADD EGGS— ONE AT A TIME. PUT IN THE REFRIGERATOR FOR A FEW HOURS. ABOUT HALF AN HOUR BEFORE ROAST BEEF IS DONE SPOON EIGHT Tbs OF FAT DRIPPINGS OR BUTTER IN A SHALLOW PAN LIKE A 9x13" PAN. SET IT IN A 450° OVEN FOR A FEW MINUTES UNTIL THE PAN IS VERY HOT. BEAT THE BATTER A BIT AND POUR INTO THE HOT PAN. BAKE AT 450° FOR 15 MINUTES AND WHEN THE PUDDING HAS RISEN, REDUCE HEAT TO 350 TO BAKE FOR 15 MINUTES.

beet
Soup
IN ROASTED
ACORN Squash

THIS IS ONE GORGEOUS SOUP AND MAKES FOR A beautiful AND DELi-CiOUS CELEbratory dish.

: FOR ROASTED SQUASH:
EiGHT INDIVIDUAL 1-1¼ lb.
ACORN SQUASH.
THREE Tbs. OIL
  ONE Tbs KOSHER SALT.

: FOR SOUP:
ONE LARGE RED ONION,
  CHOPPED
1½ Tbs OIL
FIVE MEDIUM beets (2lbs.)
PEELED AND CUT INTO 1"
  PiECES. ONE APPLE CUT IN PiECES.
TWO GARLIC CLOVES.
  MINCED
EIGHT CUPS CHICKEN STOCK
TWO Tbs. CIDER VINEGAR
  ONE Tbs PACKED brown
  SUGAR.

PREHEAT OVEN TO 375°.
CUT TOPS OFF ACORN SQUASH AND RESERVE. SCOOP OUT SEEDS AND DISCARD. CUT VERY THIN SLICE OFF bottom OF SQUASH TO CREATE A STABLE BASE. BRUSH "bowls" WiTH OiL AND SPRINKLE WITH SALT. COOK bowls AND TOPS IN THE OVEN ON TWO COOKIE SHEETS - SWITCH top AND bottom SHEET HALF WAY THROUGH COOKING. IT Should TAKE About 1¼ hours, but COOK UNTIL TENDER.

TO MAKE SOUP, COOK ONION IN OIL
IN LARGE HEAVY BOTTOMED SAUCEPAN
LIKE A DUTCH OVEN, UNTIL SOFTENED.
ADD BEETS AND APPLE AND COOK
STIRRING OCCASIONALLY FOR FIVE
MINUTES. ADD GARLIC AND COOK ABOUT
30 SECONDS. ADD BROTH AND COOK UNTIL
TENDER ABOUT 40 MINUTES. STIR IN
VINEGAR AND BROWN SUGAR. PUREE.
SEASON AND RE-HEAT IF NECESSARY.
SERVE IN SQUASH BOWLS. THIS IS ABOUT
AS PRETTY A SOUP AS YOU CAN IMAGINE.

Chlodnik

I LIKE THIS COLD SOUP. IT MAY BE JUST ME, but I find the odd INGREDIENTS MELD INTO A VERY REFRESHING AND INTERESTING SUMMER SOUP. GIVE IT A TRY AND REPORT BACK IN!!

: HALF lb. RAW PEELED AND CLEANED SHRIMP: TWO CUPS PEELED, SEEDED AND DICED CUCUMBERS: ONE tsp SALT: TWO CUPS SOUR CREAM: FIVE CUPS YOGURT OR buttermilk (I USE buttermilk).: ½ CUP SAUERKRAUT JUICE (EITHER DRAIN FROM A JAR OR blenderize SOME KRAUT WITH WATER.): TWO CLOVES GARLIC FINELY CHOPPED: HALF CUP CHOPPED FRESH FENNEL OR ONE tsp GROUND FENNEL SEED: HALF CUP SCALLIONS OR CHIVES, CUT FINE: SALT AND PEPPER TO TASTE: TWO HARD BOILED EGGS, SIEVED:

DROP SHRIMP IN boiling WATER AND bring TO boil AGAIN. IMMEDIATELY DRAIN AND PLACE Shrimp IN COLD SALTED WATER. Chill Shrimp. COMBINE CUCUMBERS AND SALT. LET STAND 30 MINUTES. DRAIN. CHOP SHRIMP.

COMBINE SOUR CREAM, YOGURT, KRAUT JUICE AND beat UNTIL SMOOTH. ADD GARLIC, FENNEL, SCALLIONS, SHRIMP AND CUCUMBER. SEASON TO TASTE. CHILL VERY WELL. SERVE GARNISHED WITH SIEVED EGG.

P.S. ANOTHER SURPRISINGLY REFRESHING soup WITH buttermilk CAN be MADE by MIXING EQUAL PARTS CHILLED TOMATO JUICE AND buttermilk. We called THIS "SUMMER SOUP" WHEN I WAS GROWING up. ADDING A DASH OF CURRY POWDER DOESN'T HURT!

FISH CHOWDER

THIS IS A WONDERFUL CHOWDER THAT WE HAVE BEEN MAKING FOR OVER THIRTY FIVE YEARS. NO ONE IS TIRED OF IT YET!

12 OUNCES CLAM BROTH
   OR FISH STOCK
3 MEDIUM POTATOES, DICED
2 CELERY STALKS, DICED
1 ONION, DICED
1 lb. WHITE FISH, CUT IN CHUNKS
2 Tbs DRIED PARSLEY
  OR HANDFUL OF FRESH
    PARSLEY, CHOPPED
1½ tsp ONION SALT
1 tsp CELERY SALT
¼ tsp BLACK PEPPER
¼ CUP BUTTER
¼ CUP FLOUR
2 CUPS HALF & HALF.

IN A HEAVY POT LIKE A DUTCH OVEN, SIMMER BROTH, POTATOES CELERY, ONIONS AND FISH TOGETHER. WHEN VEGETABLES ARE TENDER, ADD PARSLEY. ONION SALT, CELERY SALT AND BLACK PEPPER.

IN OTHER SMALL PAN, COOK BUTTER AND FLOUR TOGETHER ON LOW HEAT FOR FIVE MINUTES. STIR THIS ROUX INTO SOUP AND SIMMER UNTIL THICKENED. ADD HALF AND HALF AND SIMMER ANOTHER TEN MINUTES OR SO.

PORTUGUESE

KALE
SOUP

NONE OF MY CHILDREN
EVER COMPLAINED ABOUT KALE
WHEN IT WAS DELIVERED IN THIS
SOUP. YES, THERE WERE SOME
CHILDREN THAT ATE MORE OF
THE OTHER INGREDIENTS AND
LESS OF THE KALE, but THEY
ALL GOT USED TO KALE
because OF THIS SOUP. NOW
ONE OF THEM EVEN LIKES THE
KALE best AND PICKS THAT
OUT AFTER THE OTHERS HAVE
CHERRY PICKED THE SAUSAGE.

• • • • •

WASH AND CUT KALE INTO
DIAGONAL WIDE SLICES. WASH,
PEEL AND CHOP POTATOES
SET ASIDE.
PRICK SAUSAGE, BLANCHING
IN BOILING WATER FOR
5-10 MINUTES TO RELEASE
FAT. DRAIN AND CUT IN 1/2
INCH SLICES AND SET ASIDE.
IN A LARGE SAUCE PAN,
SAUTE ONIONS, CARROTS AND
GARLIC IN OIL AND butter
COOKING UNTIL SOFTENED

ONE lb. KALE
ONE lb. POTATOES
ONE lb. LINGUICA OR
CHORIZO OR SMOKED
SAUSAGE
ONE CUP CHOPPED ONIONS
HALF CUP CHOPPED
CARROTS.
TWO tsp. CHOPPED
GARLIC
TWO Tbs. OIL
TWO Tbs butter
TWO QUARTS CHICKEN
BROTH
THREE lbs. PEELED
SEEDED AND CHOPPED
TOMATOES.
1 1/2 CUPS COOKED KIDNEY
BEANS.

ABOUT FIVE MINUTES. ADD
 POTATOES AND BROTH.
SIMMER PARTLY COVERED
FOR 15-20 MINUTES UNTIL
POTATOES ARE COOKED. MASH
POTATOES AGAINST SIDE OF
POT, STIR IN TOMATOES
AND KIDNEY BEANS AND
SIMMER FOR 10 MINUTES.
ADD THE KALE AND
SAUSAGE AND COOK FOR
10-15 MINUTES LONGER.
SEASON WITH SALT AND
PEPPER.

KALE: IS SO BEAUTIFUL
AND EVEN IN THE NORTH
COUNTRY, WE CAN KEEP
HARVESTING IT ALMOST
TO THE NEW YEAR...
THAT IS IF THE DEER
DON'T GET THERE FIRST!!

TOMATO BISQUE WITH THYME AND BASIL

I NEVER LIKED TOMATO SOUP WHEN I
WAS A CHILD, BUT THIS IS PERHAPS
MY FAVORITE SOUP. THE THYME
IN PARTICULAR MAKES THIS SOUP
SING.

HALF CUP BUTTER • TWO Tbs. OLIVE OIL • ONE LARGE ONION
MEDIUM DICED • ONE GARLIC CLOVE, CHOPPED • 1/4 CUP FLOUR •
TWO Tbs. FRESH THYME LEAVES • TWO Tbs FRESH BASIL,
FINELY CHOPPED • SALT • BLACK PEPPER • TWO tsp. SUGAR •
THREE lbs RIPE TOMATOES (ABOUT THREE CUPS) SEEDED
AND CHOPPED. • THREE Tbs. TOMATO PASTE • FOUR
CUPS CHICKEN STOCK • ONE CUP HEAVY CREAM •

SAUTE ONION AND GARLIC IN OIL AND
BUTTER TIL GOLDEN BUT NOT BROWN. ADD
FLOUR TO MAKE A ROUX AND COOK OVER
VERY LOW HEAT FOR FIVE MINUTES. ADD
THE THYME, BASIL, SALT, PEPPER, SUGAR
TOMATOES AND TOMATO PASTE. SIMMER
TEN MINUTES. ADD STOCK AND COOK 30
MINUTES. PUREE IN BLENDER LEAVING
SMALL CHUNKS. RETURN TO HEAT AND
STIR IN CREAM.

VERMONT
CHEDDAR
Soup

10 Tbs butter
  2 cloves of garlic, minced
  1 onion, chopped
scant 1½ cups flour
3 quarts chicken stock, heated.
  1 bay leaf
    1 tsp fresh thyme
1 lb very sharp cheddar
    1 cup carrots grated
1 cup celery, minced
3 cups half and half
    (or light cream)
    salt and pepper.

Melt butter in heavy stock pot, add onions and garlic and cook until softened. Add flour and stir well. Turn heat to very low and cook for 15 minutes, stirring occasionally.

Meanwhile heat stock, then add stock a little bit at a time to flour and butter roux, stirring with whisk until smooth. Add thyme and bay leaf and cook over low heat until smooth and creamy. Grate or chop cheese into chunks and...

...add to soup, stirring until cheese is melted into soup.

In a separate saucepan cook carrots and celery in water until tender, drain and add vegetables to the soup. Add half and half and your soup is ready!

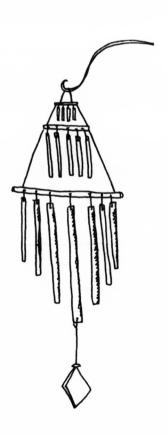

Salads and Salad Dressings

BAKERY Lane's ORIENTAL CHICKEN SALAD

A NUMBER OF OUR FAMILY'S FAVORITE RECIPES CAME FROM THE LONG GONE BAKERY LANE RESTAURANT IN MIDDLEBURY, VERMONT WHICH WAS FAMOUS IN ITS TIME FOR GREAT SOUPS AND SALADS. THIS IS A WONDERFUL SALAD TO MAKE WHEN THE GARDEN IS FLOODED WITH SPINACH AND LETTUCE.

2 lbs CHICKEN BREAST SKINNED AND BONED
1/4 CUP SOY SAUCE
2/3 CUP SALAD OIL
1 CLOVE GARLIC, PEELED
1 tsp GRATED LEMON PEEL
1/4 CUP LEMON JUICE
ONE 10oz PACKAGE RAW SPINACH
7 CUPS SHREDDED LETTUCE
3 CUPS FRESH BEAN SPROUTS
1/4 CUP TOASTED SESAME SEEDS.

CUT CHICKEN IN 2" STRIPS. ADD 1 Tbs. SOY, 2 Tbs. OIL, GARLIC AND HALF THE LEMON PEEL TO THE CHICKEN. MIX AND CHILL SEVERAL HOURS. COOK CHICKEN STRIPS IN SEVERAL Tbs. OF OIL. DISCARD GARLIC. COMBINE COOKED CHICKEN WITH REMAINING OIL, SOY SAUCE, LEMON PEEL AND LEMON JUICE.

CHOP CLEANED SPINACH AND COMBINE WITH LETTUCE AND BEAN SPROUTS. CHILL. WHEN READY TO SERVE SPRINKLE GREENS WITH SALT AND SESAME SEEDS. TOSS WITH CHICKEN MIXTURE.

broccoli
SALAD

WHEN THE BROCCOLI IS READY IN THE GARDENS,
THERE IS USUALLY WAY TOO MUCH ALL AT ONCE,
AND WE NEED TO EAT IT AT EVERY MEAL. THIS
SALAD COMES TOGETHER FAST AND USES RAW
broccoli - LOTS OF iT! THE PROPORTIONS CAN BE
PLAYED WITH i.E. YOU CAN USE MORE broccoli
AND LESS BACON AS NECESSARY TO KEEP UP
WITH ANY broccoli deluGE YOU ARE SUFFERING
FROM.

- AT LEAST ONE HEAD OF broccoli,
  CUT UP INTO bite SIZED PIECES.
- FOUR bunchinG ONIONS OR SCALLIONS
  CHOPPED • HALF CUP RAISINS PLUMPED
  IN HOT WATER • EIGHT-TEN STRIPS OF
  COOKED BACON • PECANS •

FOR SAUCE: BLEND ONE CUP HELLMAN'S MAYO
WITH HALF CUP SUGAR AND TWO Tbs. CIDER
VINEGAR.

SERVE AT ROOM TEMP, MIX-
ING AT LAST MINUTE bEFORE
SERVING TO KEEP EVERYTHING
CRISP.

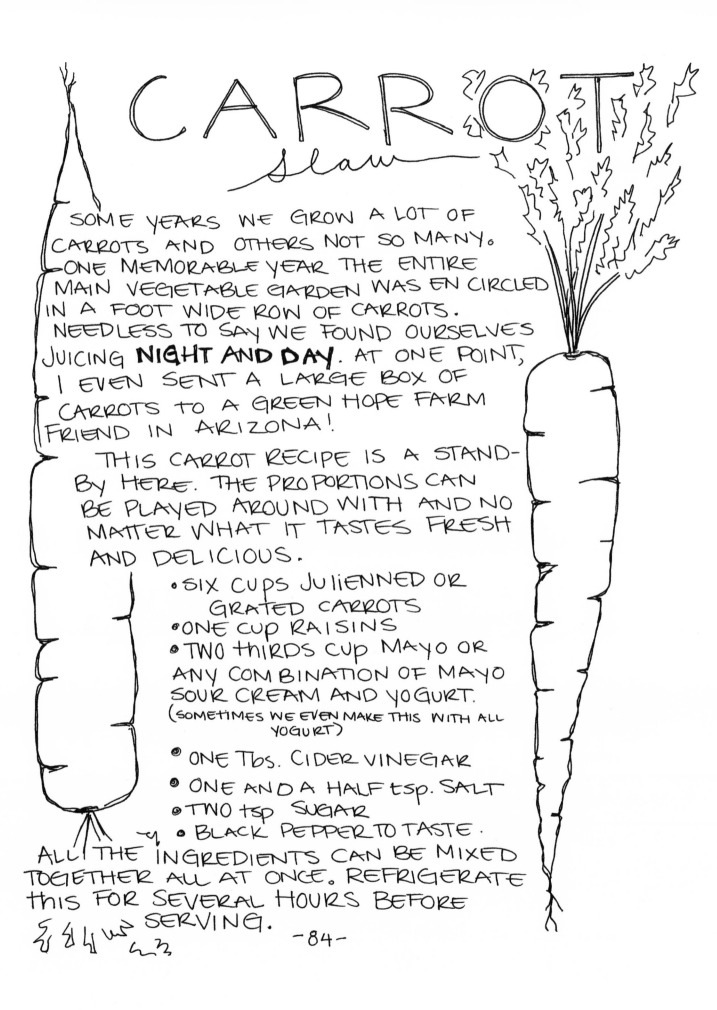

CARROT
slaw

SOME YEARS WE GROW A LOT OF CARROTS AND OTHERS NOT SO MANY. ONE MEMORABLE YEAR THE ENTIRE MAIN VEGETABLE GARDEN WAS ENCIRCLED IN A FOOT WIDE ROW OF CARROTS. NEEDLESS TO SAY WE FOUND OURSELVES JUICING **NIGHT AND DAY**. AT ONE POINT, I EVEN SENT A LARGE BOX OF CARROTS TO A GREEN HOPE FARM FRIEND IN ARIZONA!

THIS CARROT RECIPE IS A STAND-BY HERE. THE PROPORTIONS CAN BE PLAYED AROUND WITH AND NO MATTER WHAT IT TASTES FRESH AND DELICIOUS.

- SIX CUPS JULIENNED OR GRATED CARROTS
- ONE CUP RAISINS
- TWO THIRDS CUP MAYO OR ANY COMBINATION OF MAYO SOUR CREAM AND YOGURT. (SOMETIMES WE EVEN MAKE THIS WITH ALL YOGURT)
- ONE Tbs. CIDER VINEGAR
- ONE AND A HALF tsp. SALT
- TWO tsp SUGAR
- BLACK PEPPER TO TASTE.

ALL THE INGREDIENTS CAN BE MIXED TOGETHER ALL AT ONCE. REFRIGERATE THIS FOR SEVERAL HOURS BEFORE SERVING.

Chicken
SLAW

THIS IS ONE OF THOSE POTLUCK OFFERINGS THAT IS ALWAYS A HIT. YES, I KNOW IT HAS MSG IN IT. THAT'S PROBABLY WHY EVERYONE ASKS FOR THE RECIPE.

SALAD

ONE lb. BONELESS CHICKEN BREAST, COOKED AND SHREDDED

ONE lb. SHREDDED CABBAGE

FOUR GREEN ONIONS, CHOPPED.

TWO oz CHOPPED TOASTED ALMONDS OR TOASTED PECANS

TWO Tbs. SESAME SEEDS, TOASTED

ONE PACKAGE RAMEN NOODLES, CRUSHED (SAVE THE FLAVOR PACKET) BUT NOT COOKED!

CHOP ONIONS AND MIX WITH CHICKEN AND CABBAGE. ADD NOODLES, ALMONDS + SESAME SEEDS. HALF AN HOUR BEFORE SERVING ADD DRESSING.

DRESSING

HALF CUP VEGETABLE OIL

ONE Tbs. SUGAR

HALF Tsp SALT

THREE Tbs RED WINE VINEGAR

HALF Tsp. PEPPER

FLAVOR PACKET FROM NOODLES.

Creamy

Caesar DRESSING

(this one's got the ANCHOVIES IN the dressing)

▭ in FOOD PROCESSOR process:

4 ANCHOVIES
3 CLOVES GARLIC
2 Tbs. OLIVE OIL
1 tsp. WORCESTERSHIRE SAUCE
1 tsp. DIJON MUSTARD
½ tsp. Tabasco

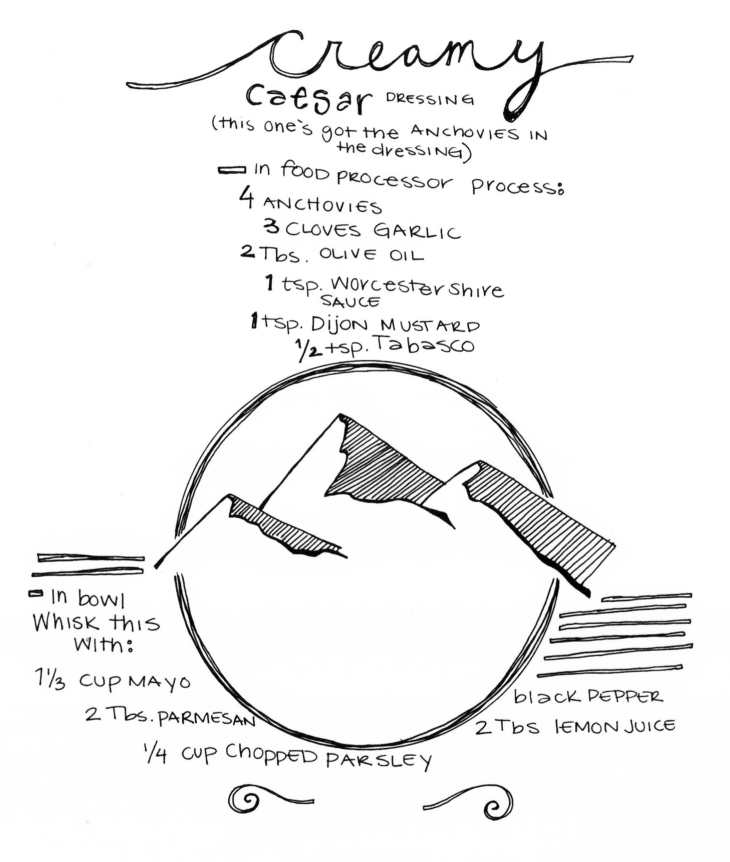

▭ in bowl Whisk this With:

1⅓ CUP MAYO
2 Tbs. PARMESAN
¼ CUP CHOPPED PARSLEY

black PEPPER
2 Tbs LEMON JUICE

Cucumber AND PINEAPPLE Salad

When Sophie Carden worked here, she brought this to an office party. We've been making it ever since. Feel free to play around with the proportions of the ingredients relative to one another—this works just as well with more pineapple and less cucumber.

— ONE CUP FRESH PINEAPPLE PIECES, CHOPPED ½ INCH DICE.

— TWO SLICING CUCUMBERS, PEELED, QUARTERED DOWN THEIR LONG SIDES THEN CHOPPED INTO ½ INCH PIECES.

— JUICE OF ONE LIME

— DRIZZLE OF HONEY — ABOUT 1-2 TBS.

— 2-3 TBS MINT LEAVES CUT INTO THIN STRIPS

— MIX ALL INGREDIENTS TOGETHER THEN CHILL IN REFRIGERATOR.

CURRIED

Red LENTIL SALAD

IN MY FIRST LARGE SCALE CATERING GIG, MY BELOVED NEIGHBOR AND FRIEND Teddy Grobe AND I FOUND OURSELVES CATERING A LARGE CHRISTMAS PARTY FOR A HIGH TECH COMPANY IN NEARBY HANOVER, NEW HAMPSHIRE. THIS RECIPE WAS the hit OF THE MEAL.

NOWADAYS, MIGUEL LIKES TO USE THE SPICE MIX FROM THIS AS A RUB FOR HIS BARBECUED BRISKETS, A TEXAS SPECIALTY HE HAS MASTERED!

DRESSING: MIX TOGETHER ... 3/4 CUP VEGETABLE OIL, 1/2 CUP RED WINE VINEGAR, 2 Tbs SUGAR, 2 tsp SALT, 2 tsp PEPPER, 1 tsp. CUMIN, 1 tsp DRY MUSTARD, 1/2 tsp TURMERIC, 1/2 tsp. MACE, 1/2 CORIANDER, 1/4 tsp. CAYENNE, 1/2 tsp. CARDAMON, 1/4 tsp CLOVES, 1/4 tsp NUTMEG, 1/4 tsp. CINNAMON, SALAD: 1 CUP DRIED CURRANTS, 1/3 CUP CAPERS, 1 1/2 CUPS CHOPPED RED ONIONS, TWO CUPS DRIED RED LENTILS.

COOK RED LENTILS IN BOILING WATER FOR 5-6 MINUTES. RINSE. DRAIN WELL AND COMBINE WITH DRESSING. LET SIT OVERNIGHT. 2 HOURS BEFORE SERVING ADD CURRANTS, CAPERS AND ONIONS.

CURRIED RICE Salad

THIS IS A RATHER 1950'S SORT OF RECIPE but WE ALL KNOW, these dishes HAVE THEIR PLACE! IT HAS BEEN MY EXPERIENCE THAT PEOPLE SCOFF THIS DOWN.

3 pkgs. CHICKEN OR HERB RICE A RONI, COOKED ACCORDING TO PACK DIRECTIONS.
 (YOU CAN USE OTHER BRANDS)

3 JARS MARINATED ARTICHOKE HEARTS IN OIL

I CAN BLACK ♡OLIVES PITTED AND CHOPPED

I CAN GREEN ♡OLIVES WITH OR WITHOUT THE PIMENTOS PITTED AND CHOPPED.

I RED ONION, FINEly CHOPPED

¼ cup OF CAPERS
 MAYONNAISE
 1 Tbs. CURRY POWDER

SALT AND PEPPER.

DRAIN AND SAVE ARTICHOKE MARINADE. ADD EQUAL PARTS OF MAYONNAISE TO THE MARINADE, ADD CURRY POWDER, SALT AND PEPPER THEN MIX WITH RICE, ARTI-CHOKES, CAPERS, ONION AND ♡OLIVES. It MAY SEEM A LITTLE GOOPY AT FIRST but AFTER REFRIGERATING THIS, THE RICE WILL SOAK up ALL THE MARINADE AND IT WILL bE A GOOD CONSISTENCY.

Dill
dressing

When the dill in the GARDEN IS YOUNG AND LEAFY, WE USE a LOT OF IT IN this CREAMY SALAD DRESSING. IT IS A GREAT DRESSING FOR A SPINACH SALAD though EQUAlly GOOD WITH LETTUCE AND CUCUMBER. IN WINTER, DRIED DIll WORKS PERFECTLY WELL.

WHISK UNTIL SMOOTH:

ONE CUP MAYONNAISE
½ CUP bUTTERMIlK
2 Tbs. OIL
2 Tbs. DIll IF DRIED
(A VERY IARGE HANDFUL IF FRESH
I USE A HAlF CUP OF CHOPPED FRESH
DILL)
½ tsp. DRY MUSTARD
TWO Tsp. ONION SALT
THREE Tbs. CIDER VINEGAR.

MAKES ABOUT TWO CUPS.

ENSALATA DI ARANCIA

EMILY DISCOVERED THIS BEAUTIFUL AND SIMPLE SALAD WHILE LIVING IN SICILY. NOW IT IS SOMETHING WE MAKE HERE TOO. I HAVE BEEN KNOWN TO HAVE IT FOR BREAKFAST!

FOUR ORANGES, PEELED AND SLICED IN ¼ INCH SLICES TO MAKE RINGS
ONE-TWO GARLIC CLOVES, MINCED
HALF ONION, DICED
FOUR TBS PARSLEY, CHOPPED
♡ OLIVE OIL
SALT
PEPPER OR CAYENNE PEPPER TO TASTE.

LAY SLICES OF ORANGE DOWN ON A PLATTER OR FLAT BOTTOM DISH. SPRINKLE GARLIC, ONIONS AND PARSLEY OVER THE ORANGES THEN DRIZZLE WITH ♡ OLIVE OIL. ADD SALT, PEPPER AND TOSS BRIEFLY.

EXORCIST: DRESSING

WAY BACK IN THE EARLY DAYS WHEN THE FARM WAS OPEN TO VISITORS, A WOMAN CAME TO THE FARM FOR A PICNIC LUNCH WITH A GREEN SALAD DRESSED WITH THIS AMAZING DRESSING. THIS IS THE RECIPE FOR THE SALAD DRESSING SHE BROUGHT THAT DAY.

THROUGHOUT THE LUNCH, SHE TOLD ME REPEATEDLY THAT SHE THOUGHT I NEEDED AN EXORCISM. EVEN AS SHE RANTED AWAY, I COULDN'T STOP THINKING ABOUT HER GREAT SALAD DRESSING, AND I ASKED HER FOR THE RECIPE. COMING UP WITH A NAME FOR THE DRESSING WAS EASY!

6 oz SALAD OIL

1 oz TAMARI SOY SAUCE

2 oz LEMON JUICE

1-2 oz TAHINI

1 oz PARSLEY

GARLIC POWDER TO TASTE

1/2 tsp MUSTARD POWDER

4 oz WATER

SALT AND PEPPER TO TASTE.

3 oz GROUND SESAME SEEDS

CAYENNE (OPTIONAL)

WHEN I MAKE THIS DRESSING I POUR THE OIL IN A LARGE MEASURING CUP THEN ADD THE RIGHT AMOUNT OF THE OTHER INGREDIENTS LIKE THE TAHINI OR LEMON JUICE BY WATCHING THE OUNCE LINE ON THE MEASURING CUP. ONCE EVERYTHING IS ASSEMBLED, ALL THE INGREDIENTS CAN BE COMBINED IN A BLENDER UNTIL CREAMY.

greek *pasta* SALAD

This has been part of countless Sheehan dinners. Feel free to add more or less vegetables and feta as you please. No matter how you make it, the teenagers will pick out the pasta leaving the vegetables for the rest of your crowd.

1 lb. ziti pasta cooked al dente

1 quart plain yogurt

1 jar Marie's creamy garlic salad dressing or equivalent.

1 tsp dried oregano

1 cucumber, halved thinly sliced

1 cup pitted Kalamata olives

At least one cup crumbled feta cheese

Cherry tomatoes

Alfalfa sprouts

2 cups of croutons

Mix yogurt, salad dressing and dried oregano together in a big bowl. Cook pasta al dente, drain and add while warm to yogurt mix. It will be soupy but noodles will soak up the dressing when it's refrigerated.

Layer on all vegetables and feta. Top with sprouts. Chill overnight if you can. Right before serving, add croutons and toss everything together.

FATTOUSH

THIS RECIPE IS FROM CATHERINE BOORADY'S FAMILY IT'S A WONDERFUL FRESH SUMMER SALAD. CATHERINE IS LEBANESE. DURING HER YEARS AT THE FARM, WE BECAME SERIOUS FANS OF HER LEBANESE FOOD. BEN CONTINUES TO GRIND HIS OWN LAMB TO MAKE CATHERINE'S KIBBEE, AND WE GROW WILD MIDDLE EASTERN OREGANO, ONE OF THE INGREDIENTS IN THE LEBANESE SPICE BLEND ZAHTAR. YOU CAN BUY ZAHTAR ONLINE IF YOU DON'T FIND IT IN YOUR GROCERY STORE.

≡ TWO Tbs. MELTED BUTTER ≡ TWO PITA BREADS ≡ 1½ CUPS CHOPPED TOMATOES ≡ ONE CUCUMBER, QUARTERED AND CUT INTO SLICES ≡ FOUR SCALLIONS, SLICED ≡ HALF CUP PARSLEY, ROUGHLY CHOPPED ≡ ¼ CUP SPEARMINT, CHOPPED ≡ THREE Tbs. ♡ OLIVE OIL ≡ JUICE OF ONE LEMON ≡ SALT AND PEPPER TO TASTE ≡ ONE - TWO Tbs ZAHTAR (CATHERINE'S RECIPE CALLS FOR ONE BUT I LIKE MORE.) ≡

SEPARATE EACH PITA BREAD INTO TWO
SIDES AND TOAST IN A 300 DEGREE
OVEN UNTIL CRISP. POUR ABOUT TWO
Tbs OF MELTED BUTTER OVER THE PITA
BREAD, BREAK INTO PIECES AND SET
ASIDE.

COMBINE CHOPPED TOMATOES, CUCUMBER,
SCALLIONS, PARSLEY AND SPEARMINT. MIX
♡OLIVE OIL, LEMON, SALT AND ZAHTAR.
TOSS WITH VEGETABLES THEN RIGHT
BEFORE SERVING ADD THE PITA PIECES
SO THEY ARE CRISPY WHEN THE SALAD
IS EATEN. YOU CAN ALSO ADD POME-
GRANATE SEEDS AND bLACK ♡OLIVES TO
THIS SALAD IF YOU WANT.

panzanella

This is another salad we have a lot in the summer. Changing the proportions of vegetables or even what vegetables are used is never a problem and whatever bread you have will work perfectly for the croutons

♡Olive oil, to generously cover the bottom of a fry pan.
Salt
Loaf of crusty whole grain bread cut into cubes — about six cups.
Four ripe tomatoes, cut into chunks.
One large cucumber skin on, cut into chunks.
Several peppers, cut in chunks
One red onion, diced.
Three Tbs. capers.
Handful of chopped basil leaves.

≡ Vinaigrette.
One tsp. or more minced garlic.
One tsp. Dijon mustard
Three Tbs. vinegar
¼ cup ♡olive oil
½ tsp. salt
¼ tsp. ground pepper.

Heat a fry pan or electric fry pan. Add a generous amount of ♡olive oil and a generous pinch of salt. Cook bread cubes until crisp and brown, turning frequently. It will probably take several batches to make all the croutons. With each batch, begin with more ♡olive oil and salt.

Because there is already ♡olive oil in the croutons, the dressing does not need as much ♡olive oil as usual. Toss all ingredients with the dressing — I like to do this right before serving so the croutons are crisp when the salad is eaten.

RICE
Salad
FROM TODAFRALI'S

THIS RECIPE CAME FROM OUR FAVORITE MOM AND POP CAFÉ IN CLAREMONT, NH, A MILL TOWN JUST SOUTH OF US. WE WENT TO TODAFRALI'S EVERY FRIDAY NIGHT WHEN THE KIDS WERE LITTLE. IT WAS A SAD DAY WHEN THE PLACE CLOSED. WE STILL MISS ALL THE FRIENDS WE MADE THERE AND THE MARVELOUS FOOD.

ONE CUP BROWN BASMATI RICE
1½ CUP COOKED BLACK BEANS
TWO TbS. ♡OLIVE OIL
ONE lb. FRESH ASPARAGUS
FOUR LARGE CLOVES GARLIC
    (MINCED)
ONE LARGE RED BELL PEPPER
    CUT INTO ½" LONG STRIPS
FIVE SCALLIONS, CHOPPED
¼ MINCED FRESH CILANTRO
⅓ CUP FRESH LIME OR LEMON
    JUICE (LIME IS BETTER)
½ tsp SALT
ONE tsp CUMIN
ONE TbS. TAMARI

COOK RICE, COMBINE WITH BLACK BEANS AND ♡OLIVE OIL. SLICE ASPARAGUS INTO DIAGONAL BITE SIZED PIECES.

STEAM ASPARAGUS FIVE MINUTES ADD TO RICE WITH GARLIC, RED PEPPER, SCALLIONS, CILANTRO. WHISK LEMON JUICE WITH SALT, CUMIN AND TAMARI THEN ADD TO REST OF SALAD

thai
NOODLES

EVERYONE SEEMS TO HAVE A
RECIPE FOR THESE AND THIS
IS OUR VERSION.

ONE lb CAPELLINI PASTA

½ CUP PEANUT OIL

½ CUP SOY SAUCE

⅔ CUP RICE VINEGAR

4 tsp. TOASTED SESAME OIL

2 Tbs. MAPLE SYRUP

2 tsp. DICED GARLIC

2 tsp. DRIED RED PEPPER FLAKES

4 tsp MINCED GINGER ROOT

1 tsp. KOSHER SALT

½ CUP CHOPPED BUNCHING
ONIONS OR SCALLIONS

½ CUP FINELY CHOPPED
CILANTRO

COOK CAPELLINI TO PACKAGE DIRECTIONS. PROCESS
EVERYTHING BUT THE CILANTRO AND BUNCHING
ONIONS IN A FOOD PROCESSOR FOR 30 SECONDS.
POUR ONTO PASTA THEN TOSS, GARNISHING WITH
THE BUNCHING ONIONS AND CILANTRO — THIS
IS BEST AT ROOM TEMPERATURE.

TORTELLINI
SALAD with BASIL
and parsley

WHILE WORKING ON THIS COOKBOOK, I RETESTED RECIPES,
EVEN TRIED AND TRUE ONES LIKE THIS ONE. THE DAY
I MADE THIS, I LEFT THE ROOM FOR A MOMENT
RIGHT AFTER ASSEMBLY AND RETURNED TO AN
EMPTY BOWL. I SOUGHT OUT ALL THE TORTELLINI
THIEVES, AND THEY GAVE THE RECIPE A THUMBS
UP. THEIR ONLY CRITICISM WAS THAT IT SHOULD BE
A DOUBLE BATCH!

8oz. Pkg. FRESH TORTELLINI
SCANT 1/4 RED WINE VINEGAR
1/4 CUP ♥OLIVE OIL
1 CLOVE GARLIC, MINCED
1 Tbs. DIJON MUSTARD
SALT & PEPPER
4 Tbs. BASIL, MINCED
2 Tbs. PARSLEY, MINCED
4 SCALLIONS, THINLY SLICED
1/4 CUP PARMESAN
    CHEESE.

COOK PASTA ACCORDING
TO PACKAGE DIRECTIONS
AND THEN BLANCH IN
COLD WATER. BLEND
TOGETHER ALL THE
REST OF THE INGRED-
IENTS EXCEPT THE
PARMESAN. ADD THE
TORTELLINI, TOSS THEN
TOP WITH THE
    PARMESAN.

VICKI'S
RUBY RED
Salad.

YIPPEE!
VICKI IS BACK
ON STAFF
JUST AS WE
GO TO PRESS!

When Vicki RAMOS—GLEN WORKED AT THE FARM SHE TAUGHT US A LOT ABOUT HOW TO USE SEAWEED! HERE IS MY FAVORITE OF HER GREAT SEAWEED RECIPES.

3 beets GRATED OR SLICED and then STEAMED FIVE MINUTES OR UNTIL TENDER.

½ cup ARAME SOAKED IN ONE CUP WATER FOR FIVE MINUTES then DRAINED.

4 RED CABBAGE LEAVES SLICED thin INTO BITE SIZED PIECES

ONE RED ONION SLICED OR DICED

ONE BUNCH RADISHES, SLICED

ONE Tbs. EXTRA VIRGIN OLIVE OIL

ONE Tbs. RICE VINEGAR

ONE Tbs. tamari OR UMEBOSHI VINEGAR.

TOSS ALL INGREDIENTS TOGETHER

VICKI OFTEN ADDS SOBA NOODLES TO THIS SALAD

BASMATI
RICE
WITH
Cumin
JEERA RICE

THIS IS OUR "GOTO" RECIPE FOR RICE WHETHER THE MEAL IS AN INDIAN FEAST OR NOT.

1 ½ CUP UNCOOKED BASMATI RICE
3 Tbs. VEGETABLE OIL
½ tsp. CUMIN SEEDS
2×2 INCH CINNAMON STICKS
4 WHOLE CLOVES.
1 ¼ tsp. SALT

WASH RICE IN THREE CHANGES OF COLD WATER AND THEN SOAK FOR 15-20 MINUTES WITH FRESH COLD WATER. HEAT OIL IN SAUCEPAN AND WHEN HOT ADD CUMIN, CINNAMON AND CLOVES. COOK FOR FIVE MINUTES, THEN ADD THE RICE, SALT, AND 2½ CUPS WATER. COVER AND BRING TO A BOIL. STIR ONCE. TURN THE HEAT DOWN TO LOW AND SIMMER GENTLY, COVERED, FOR 10-12 MINUTES OR UNTIL ALL WATER IS ABSORBED.

THIS RECIPE CAME FROM OUR IRISH COUSIN CATHERINE O'TOOLE PRYCE WHO SERVED IT TO US IN THE SUMMER OF 2005 IN HER LOVELY KITCHEN IN CONNEMARA.

[IT CAN BE USED AS A DIP, VEGETABLE SIDE DISH, OR EVEN AS A PASTA SAUCE.]

butterbeans
WITH
rosemary
AND
SUN DRIED TOMATOES

○ 14 OUNCE TIN BUTTERBEAN OR CANNELLINI BEAN (ANY KIND OF WHITE BEAN)

○ 3 Tbs OLIVE OIL

○ 3 Tbs SUN DRIED TOMATOES CHOPPED (IF YOU CAN FIND SEMI SUN DRIED, THEY ARE SOFTER)

○ GENEROUS tsp OF CHOPPED FRESH ROSEMARY.

○ SALT AND PEPPER TO TASTE

DRAIN BEANS. MIX ALL INGREDIENTS IN A SAUCEPAN AND HEAT UP GENTLY. THEN SET IN A BOWL TO HAVE FLAVORS INFUSE. SERVE AT ROOM TEMPERATURE.

COSTA RICAN
RICE.

JEISON CAME FROM THE OSA PENINSULA OF COSTA RICA TO LIVE ON OUR HILL TOP FOR SEVERAL YEARS. ON HIS WAY HOME FROM WORK HE WOULD STOP IN AT THE FARM FOR A CHAT OR A MEAL. THESE VISITS WERE LIKE SUN-SHINE AS NO ONE COULD BRI-GHTEN SPIRITS LIKE JEISON. HE LOVED TO COOK FOR US AND ALWAYS INCLUDED THIS RICE IN HIS MENUS.

3-4 TBS. BUTTER

ONE YELLOW ONION CUT INTO HALF MOON SLICES.

THREE CLOVES GARLIC, DICED

ONE AND A HALF CUPS RICE

THREE CUPS WATER

ONE TSP. SALT.

HEAT BUTTER THEN COOK ONIONS ON MEDIUM LOW FOR TEN MINUTES. ADD GARLIC THEN COOK A FURTHER FIVE MINUTES. ADD RICE AND SALT, COOKING ON MEDIUM HIGH FOR A MINUTE. ADD WATER AND BRING TO BOIL. BOIL FOR FIVE MINUTES THEN TURN TO LOW, COVER RICE AND COOK 15 MINUTES UNTIL LIGHT AND FLUFFY.

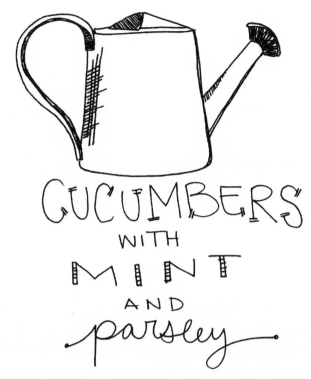

CUCUMBERS
WITH
MINT
AND
parsley

THIS IS A SURPRISINGLY DELICIOUS THING TO THROW TOGETHER WHEN YOU FIND A BEHEMOTH CUCUMBER OR TWO HIDING BENEATH THE CUCUMBER VINES. YOU CAN ALSO ADD MONSTER ZUCCHINIS TO THIS.

TWO OR THREE OVERSIZED CUCUMBERS
SALT
SMALL BUNCH OF MINT
SMALL BUNCH OF PARSLEY
RED ONION, DICED
RED WINE VINEGAR
OLIVE OIL

PEEL, QUARTER AND DE-SEED YOUR BEHEMOTH CUCUMBERS THEN CUT THEM INTO SMALL CUBES. SALT THE CUCUMBER WITH AMPLE SALT - TWO tsp. IS NOT TOO MUCH. CHOP UP THE MINT AND PARSLEY AND ADD THIS TO THE CUCUMBER WITH RED ONION. ADD RED WINE VINEGAR AND OLIVE OIL AS YOU MIGHT TO A SALAD.

DILLY beans

If you have never made pickles, these are a great place to start. If you don't grow dill, you can substitute dill seeds

▭ ▭ ▭

Pack beans lengthwise into six hot pint jars. Leave 1/4 inch head space at top. To each pint add 1/4 tsp cayenne, 1 clove garlic and 1 head dill or 1 tsp. dill seeds. Boil water, vinegar and salt together then pour into jars, leaving 1/4 inch at the top. Process in a boiling water bath for ten minutes. Let stand for two weeks before serving.

▭ ▭ ▭

3 lbs string beans, trimmed and straight

1 1/2 tsp cayenne

6 cloves garlic

6 heads dill or 6 tsp dill seeds

3 1/2 cups water

3 1/2 cups vinegar, cider or white

1/3 cup salt (pickling salt is best!)

▭ ▭ ▭

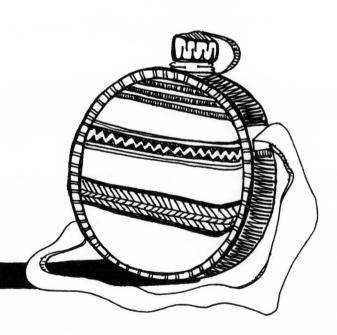

MEXICAN :RICE:

2 Tbs. butter

1 YELLOW ONION, DICED

3 CLOVES GARLIC, DICED

2 CUPS RICE

LARGE CAN DICED TOMATOES

CHICKEN STOCK

1 tsp. SALT

BEGIN by PUT-
TING RICE IN
COLD WATER
TO SOAK.
SET ASIDE

HEAT BUTTER AND
COOK ONIONS IN
BUTTER TEN MINUTES.
ADD GARLIC AND
COOK A FURTHER FIVE
MINUTES

POUR CAN OF TOMATOES
IN QUART MEASURING
CUP AND FILL TO QUART
LINE WITH CHICKEN
STOCK.

DRAIN RICE AND ADD TO POT. FRY RICE FOR FIVE MINUTES ON
MEDIUM HIGH. ADD TOMATO LIQUID, BOIL FOR FIVE MINUTES
THEN TURN DOWN TO LOW, COVER THE POT AND COOK FOR
TEN - FIFTEEN MINUTES UNTIL LIGHT AND FLUFFY.

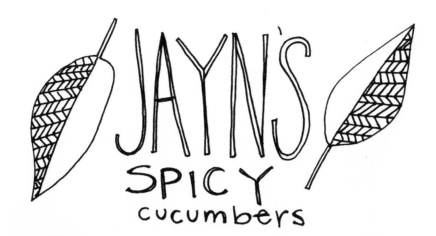

JAYN'S SPICY cucumbers

JAYN BIER WORKED AT THE FARM IN ITS EARLY DAYS. SHE TAUGHT ME A LOT ABOUT CARING FOR THE TROPICAL PLANTS IN OUR GREEN HOUSE, ESPECIALLY ENCOURAGING ME TO BE A FEARLESS PRUNER. WE ALSO SPENT A LOT OF TIME TYING UP LEGGY ROSES TOGETHER. NOWADAYS, I THINK OF HER OFTEN WHILE I WRESTLE AND ROPE IN MORE AND MORE ROSES IN OUR EVER EXPANDING ROSE GARDEN.

ONE LARGE CUCUMBER OR TWO SMALL ONES ✿ ONE TSP SALT ✿ ONE TBS SOY SAUCE ✿ ONE AND A HALF TSP VINEGAR ✿ HALF TSP. SUGAR ✿ TWO TBS. CHOPPED GARLIC ✿ ONE TSP. CHILI OIL OR TABASCO SAUCE ✿ ONE AND ONE HALF TSP BROWN BEAN SAUCE ✿ ONE TSP SZECHUAN PEPPER CORNS ✿ ONE TBS. SESAME OIL ✿

PEEL CUCUMBER AND CUT LENGTHWISE INTO TWO SECTIONS. SCOOP OUT SEEDS WITH A SPOON AND CUT SECTIONS INTO PIECES 3/4" WIDE AND 1/4" THICK. PUT CUCUMBER SLICES IN A BOWL, ADD SALT AND TOSS THOROUGHLY. LET STAND FOR ABOUT AN HOUR.

WASH CUCUMBER WITH COLD WATER DRAIN AND PAT DRY. COMBINE CU-CUMBER WITH ALL THE OTHER INGREDIENTS AND MIX THOROUGHLY. MARINATE AT LEAST THREE HOURS OR OVERNIGHT.

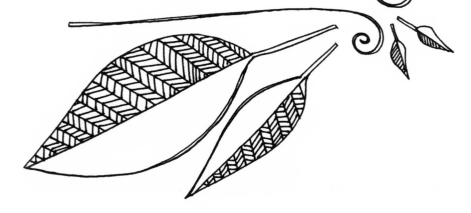

Mrs. Chalupa's
~Refrigerated~
Pickles

My childhood neighbor, Jody Newmyer, gave me both the recipe for Nebraska Thresher's Cake and this, her mother. Mrs. Chalupa's bread and butter pickle recipe. Jody grew up in almost pioneer conditions on a small farm near Wilber, Nebraska.

Because the recipe makes a lot of pickles, I have given a version for a smaller batch in parenthesis after each ingredient. The smaller batch will still fill a gallon jar with pickles.

25 not too large cucumbers, washed and sliced thinly (8 for smaller batch)
3 medium onions peeled and thinly sliced (1)
4 cups cider vinegar (1 1/3 cups)
5 cups sugar (1 2/3 cups)
1 tsp turmeric (1/3 tsp)
1 1/2 tsp celery seed (1/2 tsp)
1 1/2 tsp mustard seed (1/2 tsp)

Mix everything but cucumbers and onions and pour over cucumbers and onions. Toss slightly and place in glass jars. Store in refrigerator. These are so easy and keep well.

PARSLEY AND ITS RISE TO STARDOM HERE AT GHF.

WHEN I WAS YOUNGER, I COULDN'T REALLY BE BOTHERED WITH GOING OUT TO THE GARDENS TO GET PARSLEY FOR A DISH. I MEAN, WASN'T IT REALLY ONLY A GARNISH?

NOW I AM CRAZY ABOUT PARSLEY AND THINK IT IS ONE OF THE BEST VEGETABLES WE GROW. I PUT IT IN EVERYTHING AND GROW A LOT OF DIFFERENT KINDS OF PARSLEY. WE EVEN HAD A TASTE TEST ONE SUMMER, GROWING then tASTING All SORTS OF PARSLEY to SEE WHICH ONES WE LIKED bEST. A VARIETY CALLED KRAUSA WAS the HANDS DOWN tAStE tESt WINNER SO WE AlWAYS grow that ONE alonG With ABOUT HAlF A DOZEN OTHER VARIETIES.

THESE DAYS, PARSLEY HAS FOUND A SERIOUS PLACE IN OUR HEARTS, AND I HAPPILY SPRINT OUT TO THE GARDENS TO PICK SOME FOR ANY DISH WHERE PARSLEY IS CALLED FOR AND SOME WHERE IT IS NOT.

CLASSIC

pesto

TEDDY MADE THIS PESTO WITH
PINE NUTS but I PREFER
WALNUTS. THE CHOICE IS YOURS.

2 cups BASIL LEAVES, PACKED
5 CLOVES GARLIC
1 CUP WALNUTS
1 CUP ♡OLIVE OIL
1 CUP PARMESAN CHEESE,
GRATED
1/4 CUP ROMANO CHEESE
SALT AND PEPPER TO TASTE

COMBINE THE BASIL, GARLIC AND WALNUTS
IN A FOOD PROCESSOR AND CHOP. POUR
♡OLIVE OIL THROUGH FEEDING TUBE IN A
STEADY STREAM. TURN OFF MOTOR AND ADD
CHEESES. THIS FREEZES WELL.

CILANTRO

PESTO

AFTER NUMEROUS TRIAL
BATCHES OF THIS PESTO,
WE ALL AGREED THIS
VERSION WAS OUR FAVORITE.

- FOUR CUPS FRESH CILANTRO, -
  STALKS INCLUDED
- ONE JALAPENO, SEEDED -
  AND ROUGH CHOPPED
- FIVE CLOVES GARLIC -
- HALF CUP WALNUTS -
  - HALF CUP PARMESAN -
  CHEESE
- HALF tsp. SALT -
  - HALF CUP OLIVE -
  OIL

IN A FOOD PROCESSOR, FINELY CHOP EVERY-
THING BUT THE OIL. ADD THE OIL AND MIX
AGAIN. THIS CAN BE USED AS A SALSA OR
A PESTO. IT IS GREAT IN QUESADILLAS. —113—

GARLIC SCAPES
pesto

BUNCH OF GARLIC SCAPES, ENOUGH TO MAKE 1½ CUP WHEN GROUND UP.
GENEROUS HANDFUL OF WALNUTS.
3/4 CUP ♡ OLIVE OIL
1 CUP PARMESAN CHEESE
1/4 CUP ROMANO CHEESE

THE BEAUTIFUL CURLY GREEN SHOOTS ON THE TOP OF GARLIC PLANTS ARE CALLED GARLIC SCAPES. THEY HAVE TO BE CUT OFF THE GARLIC PLANTS SO THAT ALL THE PLANTS' ENERGY GOES INTO THE GARLIC CLOVES AND NOT INTO THE FLOWER. WE CUT OUR SCAPES IN LATE JUNE HERE AT THE FARM.

I NEVER QUITE KNEW WHAT TO DO WITH ALL THE GARLIC SCAPES WE HAD. THIS YEAR, WHEN I POSTED A PHOTOGRAPH ON FACEBOOK OF GARLIC SCAPES, SOMEONE SUGGESTED I TRY GARLIC SCAPE PESTO. I CAN CERTAINLY SEE WHY THIS PESTO IS ALL THE RAGE. IN FACT, WE WERE ALL VERY DISAPPOINTED TO SEE THE LAST OF THE GARLIC SCAPES AS THIS DELICIOUS ZESTY PESTO WENT ON PIZZAS, INTO OMELETS, SPREAD ON CHEESE AND CRACKERS EVEN SPOONED INTO PEOPLE'S MOUTHS. IT IS THAT GOOD!!

FIRST OF ALL, DON'T PAY TOO MUCH ATTENTION TO THE PROPORTIONS HERE. YOU CAN'T MESS THIS UP NO MATTER HOW YOU PUT THESE INGREDIENTS TOGETHER! WHEN READY TO MAKE YOUR PESTO, CUT THE IMMATURE BLOSSOM HEADS OFF THE GARLIC SCAPES. THESE ARE PAPERY WHITISH DOMES AT THE TOP OF THE SCAPE. USING SCISSORS, CUT THE SCAPES INTO PIECES RIGHT INTO THE BOWL OF YOUR FOOD PROCESSOR. ADD A GENEROUS HANDFUL OF WALNUTS OR NUTS OF YOUR PREFERENCE. BLITZ UNTIL THE SCAPES ARE CHOPPED FINE BUT NOT A SMOOTH PASTE. YOU WANT THE PESTO TO HAVE SOME TEXTURE. ADD ♡ OLIVE OIL AND PARMESAN AND ROMANO AND BRIEFLY MIX. THIS IS READY FOR YOUR SPOONS!

RED Shiso WITH CUCUMBER

NO OTHER PLANT AT GREEN HOPE FARM HAS GIVEN MORE GENEROUSLY OR BEEN MORE IMPORTANT TO OUR MISSION THAN RED SHISO, THE PLANT WE USE TO MAKE OUR FLOWER ESSENCE STABILIZER.

RED SHISO WAS FIRST BROUGHT TO MY ATTENTION BY MAYME NODA. WHEN I FIRST MOVED TO MERIDEN IN THE LATE 70'S, MAYME WAS ONE OF THE MOVERS AND SHAKERS IN THE VILLAGE. IN OUR TINY TOWN OF 1,750 PEOPLE. THERE WERE PLAYS, THERE WERE RALLIES, THERE WERE PARTIES, THERE WERE CONCERTS AND MAYME WAS ALWAYS IN THE CENTER OF EVERYTHING. SHE SHARED THIS RECIPE WITH ONE AND ALL, INSISTING ON CERTAIN STANDARDS IF WE WERE TO EVEN BEGIN TO APPROXIMATE THE dishes OF HER JAPANESE ROOTS.

MAYME'S FIRST RULE: THE CUCUMBERS MUST BE SLICED PAPER THIN. (EVEN IF THIS MEANS DANGER TO ONE'S KNUCKLES...)

MAYME'S SECOND RULE: DON'T SKIMP ON THE SUGAR. SHE SAID JAPANESE COOKING WAS VERY SWEET AND THE SUGAR MADE THE RECIPE TRUE TO THE ORIGINAL.

MAYME DID NOT HOWEVER EXPLAIN PROPORTIONS SO THIS RECIPE IS A BIT VAGUE. IT IS NONETHELESS DELICIOUS! I USUALLY SLICE TWO OR THREE CUCUMBERS THEN A HANDFUL OF RED SHISO LEAVES. THE CONTRASTING COLORS ARE VERY PRETTY.

CUCUMBERS, PEELED, SEEDED IF LARGE, THEN SLICED EXTREMELY THIN.
RED SHISO LEAVES, RICE VINEGAR AND WHITE SUGAR.

TAKE THE CUCUMBER SLICES, SALT THEM THEN SQUEEZE OUT THE WATER. ADD RED SHISO CUT IN EXTREMELY THIN STRIPS ADD TO THIS EQUAL PARTS RICE VINEGAR AND SUGAR. THE RED SHISO HAS A WONDERFUL FRESH TASTE AND MAKES THIS INTO A BEAUTIFUL AND SPECIAL DISH.

ROASTED
NEW POTATOES
WITH
MINT.

ABOUT NOW YOU PROBABLY THINK EVERY DISH
WE MAKE HERE HAS MINT IN IT. WELL, WE DO
HAVE AN ENORMOUS BED OF MINT AND THIS
DOES KEEP US MOTIVATED TO THINK OF
THINGS TO DO WITH THIS ZESTY FRIEND.
HERE'S A POTATO DISH THAT USES LOTS
OF MINT.

FIVE lbs. NEW POTATOES, SKINS ON
FIVE-ten CLOVES OF GARLIC, FINELY MINCED
1¼ CUP OLIVE OIL
TWO CUPS CHOPPED MINT
ONE Tbs. SALT
PEPPER TO TASTE.

WASH AND PRICK THE
POTATOES WITH A FORK SO
NONE OF THEM EXPLODE.
PUT ON A BIG COOKIE SHEET
AND BAKE AT 350° FOR
TWO HOURS. REMOVE FROM
OVEN AND CUT EACH POTATO
IN HALF. TOSS THE POTATOES
WITH THE GARLIC, OIL, MINT AND
SALT. LET EVERYTHING SIT, TOSSING
OCCASIONAlly FOR HALF AN HOUR.

SADZA

CALLED FUFU IN KENYA, UGALI IN NIGERIA AND PAP IN SOUTH AFRICA, SADZA IS PART OF MOST EVERY MEAL THEMBI COOKS FOR HER HUSBAND AND FOUR SONS. WHEN LIZZY AND MIGUEL GOT MARRIED, THEMBI BROUGHT A BIG DISH OF SADZA TO THE WEDDING PARTY. SHE SAID IT WAS FOR MIGUEL AND ALL HIS INTERNATIONAL FRIENDS WHO HAD LIVED AND WORKED IN KENYA. THE REST OF US WERE ALSO DELIGHTED TO GET THIS TASTE OF THEMBI'S HOME. SHE USUALLY PAIRS SADZA WITH KALE, CABBAGE BEANS AND STEWS.

STAFF GODDESS, THEMBI MUHLAURI COMES TO US FROM ZIMBABWE. LEAVING BEHIND A VERY BUSTLING CITY LIFE SURROUNDED BY FAMILY IN TROPICAL HARARE, THEMBI HAS CHEERFULLY EMBRACED HER NEW LIFE IN OUR VERY TINY, VERY COLD AND VERY RURAL VILLAGE.

TEN CUPS WATER
THREE CUPS CORN MEAL
HALF CUP WATER
THREE MORE CUPS CORN MEAL.

BRING THE WATER TO A BOIL ON MEDIUM HEAT. MIX THREE CUPS OF THE CORNMEAL WITH AN HALF CUP OF WATER TO MAKE A SMOOTH PASTE THEN POUR INTO THE BOILING WATER. STIR UNTIL A SOFT SMOOTH PASTE FORMS. LET SIMMER FOR FIVE MINUTES THEN ADD THREE CUPS OF CORNMEAL BIT BY BIT UNTIL IT STARTS TO BECOME THICKER AND THICKER LIKE MASHED POTATOES. TURN HEAT TO LOW UNTIL YOU ARE READY TO SERVE. THEMBI SAYS THIS SERVES 6-8 PEOPLE.

SOUBISE

This is a JULIA CHILD RECIPE that WAS A Staple At ALL fancy family dinners when I Was growing UP. NOW that food processors can be USED to Slice the onions, this recipe IS A SNAP to MAKE.

- ½ CUP RICE -
- FOUR Tbs. butter -
- 6-7 CUPS SLICED ONIONS -

Thinly Slice onions. Boil rice FOR 5 MINUTES. DRAIN IMMEDIATELY. FOAM butter IN AN OVENPROOF CASSEROLE dish. ADD RICE AND ONIONS. COVER AND COOK 1 hour AT 300° STIRRING OCCASIONAILY.

Spicy
CAULIFLOWER AND POTATOES
— MASALEDAR GOBI ALOO —

¼ CUP VEGETABLE OIL

1 MEDIUM ONION, CHOPPED

2 LARGE POTATOES, PEELED AND CUT INTO SMALL PIECES

⅛ TO 1 tsp. CAYENNE (DEPENDING ON HOW HOT YOU WANT THIS)

¼ CUP LEMON JUICE

1 tsp. SALT

¼ tsp. TURMERIC

1 MEDIUM CAULIFLOWER, WASHED AND CUT INTO FLORETS

½ JALAPENO OR 1 HOT FRESH GREEN CHILI IF DESIRED

½ CUP PLAIN YOGURT MIXED WITH ½ CUP WATER

1 tsp. MUSTARD SEEDS

COOK ONION IN OLIVE OIL UNTIL IT BEGINS TO BROWN. STIR IN POTATOES AND COOK UNTIL THEY ALSO BEGIN TO BROWN. ADD RED PEPPER, LEMON JUICE, SALT AND TURMERIC. COOK FOR A COUPLE OF MINUTES THEN ADD CAULIFLOWER ADDITIONAL CHILIS IF USING, YOGURT AND WATER. STIR WELL. CONTINUE COOKING ABOUT 20-30 MINUTES UNTIL VEGETABLES ARE TENDER.

Spinach CROQuettes

3/4 cup MELTED Butter.

2 pkgs Chopped FROZEN spinach, drained or two bunches FRESH that have been steamed AND CHOPPED.

3 cups herb stuffing mix Like pepperidge FARM

1 cup finely Chopped ONIONS

1/2 cup PARMESAN cheese.

4 eggs, beaten

1/2 tsp. garlic POWDER, SALT & THyME

MIX ALL ingredients together then refrigerate for three hours or overnight. ROll into 1" balls AND BAKE AT 350° for 20 minutes.

braised beef
with guinness

We have MANY RELATIVES IN CONNEMARA
ON THE WEST COAST OF IRELAND HENCE
OUR TRIPS to IRELAND AND OUR FLOWER
ESSENCES FROM THIS WONDERFUL PLACE.
THIS IS A RECIPE WE GOT IN IRELAND
1998. THE GUINNESS AND THE ORANGE
PEEL GIVE THE STEW A LOVELY AND DIFF-
ERENT FLAVOR.

TWO Tbs. ♡OLIVE OIL
  THREE lbs. STEWING beef CUT IN CUBES
ONE LARGE ONION, CHOPPED
  ONE lb CARROTS, CUT IN FINGERS
SIX CLOVES GARLIC PEELED but WHOLE.
  TWO Tbs. FLOUR
  ONE Tbs TOMATO PUREE
    1 1/4 PINTS GUINNESS

ONE BOUQUET GARNI WITH 3 bay LEAVES
2 SPRIGS OF ROSEMARY, 2 SPRIGS
THYME, PARSLEY AND THREE STRIPS
OF ORANGE PEEL TIED TOGETHER
WITH A STRING.
SALT & PEPPER.

OPTIONAL: 7oz WHOLE PITTED PRUNES
SOAKED OVERNIGHT AND DRAINED

PREHEAT OVEN TO 300 DEGREES.

HEAT OIL IN A HEAVY BOTTOMED CASSEROLE. SEAR THE MEAT BRIEFLY ON ALL SIDES. REMOVE. ADD ONION, CARROTS AND GARLIC AND LET THEM COLOR BEFORE ADDING FLOUR. ADD TOMATO PUREE AND RETURN MEAT TO CASSEROLE. POUR IN GUINNESS SLOWLY STIRRING TO ALLOW LIQUID TO THICKEN. BURY THE BOUQUET GARNI IN LIQUID AND BRING TO BOILING POINT. SEASON WITH SALT AND PEPPER AND PUT IN OVEN FOR 1 1/2 HOURS.

ADD SOAKED PRUNES IF YOU ARE USING THEM AND COOK FOR 30 MINUTES MORE. DISCARD BOUQUET GARNI BEFORE SERVING.

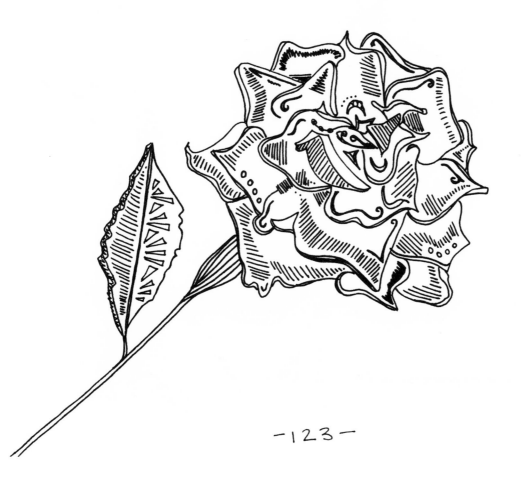

buffalo CHICKEN MACARONI AND Cheese

Ben also makes a buffalo chicken pizza with somewhat the same ingredients. Here the delivery device for the spicy chicken is macaroni and cheese.

COMBINE CORNSTARCH, MILK AND EGGS IN A BOWL AND WHISK WELL AND SET ASIDE. COOK PASTA ACCORDING TO PACKAGE DIRECTIONS IN A LARGE HEAVY BOTTOMED POT LIKE A DUTCH OVEN. DRAIN AND RESERVE 1 CUP OF THE PASTA COOKING WATER. RETURN PASTA TO COOKING POT AND ADD PASTA WATER, EGG MIXTURE CHEESE AND HOT SAUCE. COOK OVER LOW HEAT, STIRRING CONSTANTLY UNTIL CHEESE IS MELTED AND SAUCE IS CREAMY AND SMOOTH. STIR IN CHICKEN AND HALF THE SCALLIONS. PUT IN A SERVING BOWL AND GARNISH WITH blue CHEESE AND REST OF THE SCALLIONS.

- 4 tsp. CORNSTARCH
- 2 CANS (12 oz. EACH) EVAPORATED MILK
- 4 EGGS
- 1 lb. SHAPED PASTA OF YOUR CHOICE
- 24 oz MEDIUM SHARP CHEDDAR CHEESE, GRATED - OTHERS WORK WELL TOO!!
- ½ CUP HOT SAUCE (WE USE FRANKS)
- 2-4 CUPS CUT UP COOKED CHICKEN MEAT - THIS IS A GOOD DISH TO MAKE WITH LEFT-OVER ROAST CHICKEN.
- 1 CUP SLICED SCALLIONS
- 1 CUP BLUE CHEESE, CRUMBLED.

CATHERINE'S
Corn Pone

WHEN CATHERINE
BARRITT WORKED
HERE, OUR OFFICE
WAS ONE tiny
ROOM. THIS MEANT
WE COULD ALWAYS
HEAR HER WONDER-
FUL INFECTIOUS
LAUGH. HERE'S A
RECIPE SHE SHARED
WITH THE OFFICE
DURING THOSE EARLY
DAYS.

4 CUPS VERY JUICY COOKED
AND SEASONED BEANS.

2 CUPS CORNMEAL
2 tsp BAKING SODA
1 tsp SALT
1 QUART BUTTERMILK
2 EGGS, SLIGHTLY BEATEN
1/4 CUP MELTED BUTTER.

COMBINE CORNBREAD INGRED-
IENTS. POUR OVER HOT BEANS.
BAKE ON TOP RACK OF OVEN
UNTIL BREAD IS RICH GOLDEN
AND SIDES PULL AWAY - 30
MINUTES AT 400 DEGREES.
FOR COOKING PAN YOU CAN
USE A 9 X 13 PAN OR bIG
DUTCH OVEN. THIS IS GOOD
WITH THE ADDITION OF SOME
COOKED GROUND BEEF IN
THE BEANS.

Chicken BARBEQUE SAUCE

THIS RECIPE FOR AN ALTERNATIVE TO TOMATO BASED BBQ SAUCE CAME FROM MY DEAR STEP-GRANDMOTHER BOBBY.

ONE CUP SHERRY

HALF CUP OLIVE OIL

ONE LARGE ONION, CHOPPED

ONE Tbs. WORCESTERSHIRE SAUCE

ONE tsp. SOY SAUCE

ONE tsp. LEMON JUICE

ONE tsp. POWDERED GARLIC

ONE tsp. THYME

ONE tsp. OREGANO

ONE tsp. ROSEMARY NEEDLES

ONE tsp. MARJORAM

TWO CHICKENS CUT UP

USE TO MARINATE THE CHICKEN BEFORE COOKING. YOU CAN ALSO BASTE THE CHICKEN WITH THIS WHILE BARBECUING.

Chicken Curry WITH CREAM OF COCONUT

THIS IS A GREAT RECIPE FOR A PARTY OR BIG DINNER. EVERYONE SEEMS TO LIKE IT AND WANT THE RECIPE.

HALF CUP FLOUR
SALT AND PEPPER
5 Tbs. BUTTER
ONE ONION CHOPPED
2 CLOVES GARLIC, MINCED.
2 GREEN PEPPERS, SEEDED AND DICED
3 Tbs. CURRY POWDER
ONE CAN 15 oz TOMATOES.
ONE CAN 15 oz CREAM OF COCONUT (NOT COCONUT MILK BUT BRAND LIKE COCO LOPEZ)
DASH WORCESTERSHIRE SAUCE AND TOBASCO SAUCE
HALF CUP DRIED CURRANTS.

3 lbs. CHICKEN PIECES THIGHS OR BREAST.

COAT CHICKEN WITH FLOUR, SALT AND PEPPER. BROWN IN 3 Tbs. BUTTER. REMOVE FROM SKILLET. ADD REMAINING 2 Tbs. OF BUTTER AND SAUTE ONIONS, GARLIC AND GREEN PEPPERS UNTIL SOFT. ADD CURRY POWDER AND SAUTE A FEW MORE MINUTES. ADD THE TOMATOES AND THE CREAM OF COCONUT AND DASH OF TABASCO AND WORCESTERSHIRE SAUCE. STIR IN CURRANTS.

ARRANGE CHICKEN IN CASSEROLE DISH AND POUR OVER SAUCE. BAKE IN 350 DEGREE OVEN, COVERED, UNTIL CHICKEN IS TENDER ABOUT AN HOUR. I FIND IT OFTEN NEEDS MORE THAN AN HOUR.

CHILI CHEESE CASSEROLE

THIS puffy, Mild mannered DELIGHT IS A RECIPE FROM SHARI SCOTT, AN EARLY FRIEND OF GREEN HOPE FARM. SHARI SET UP OUR FIRST COMPUTER PROGRAM FOR OUR MAILING LIST WAY BACK WHEN I WAS SURE WE WOULD NEVER REALLY NEED COMPUTERS. THANKS SHARI FOR BEING MORE CLUED IN THAN ME!

TWO 4 oz CANS GREEN CHILIS SEEDED AND CHOPPED

1 lb. EACH MONTEREY JACK AND CHEDDAR CHEESE, GRATED

FOUR EGG WHITES

FOUR EGG YOLKS

1/2 tsp. SALT

2/3 CUP MILK

1 Tbs. FLOUR

1/4 tsp. PEPPER

THREE MEDIUM TOMATOES SLICED.

COMBINE GRATED CHEESES AND CHILIS IN LARGE BOWL. TURN INTO WELL BUTTERED 2 QUART CASSEROLE DISH.

IN SEPARATE BOWL, BEAT EGG WHITES UNTIL STIFF.

IN YET ANOTHER BOWL, COMBINE AND MIX WELL THE YOLKS, MILK, FLOUR, SALT AND PEPPER. USING A RUBBER SPATULA GENTLY FOLD EGG WHITES INTO YOLK MIXTURE.

USING FORK OOZE EGG MIXTURE ONTO CHEESE AND CHILI MIX HELPING IT TO SOAK IN.

BAKE AT 325 DEGREES FOR 30 MINUTES. ARRANGE TOMATO SLICES AROUND EDGE OF THE CASSEROLE AND RETURN TO OVEN FOR ANOTHER 30 MINUTES OR UNTIL KNIFE INSERTED IN MIDDLE COMES OUT CLEAN.

CODFISH CAKES
WITH
Lemon caper tartar
SAUCE

THIS RECIPE MAKES A LOT OF CODFISH CAKES BUT NOBODY EVER COMPLAINS AS THEY MAKE EXCELLENT LEFTOVERS FOR BREAKFAST, LUNCH OR DINNER. THE TARTAR SAUCE IS ALSO VERY GOOD AND CAN BE USED WITH OTHER FISH DISHES.

THREE lbs. CODFISH
12 MEDIUM POTATOES
TWO ONIONS, FINELY CHOPPED
ONE CUP CHOPPED FLAT LEAFED PARSLEY
FIVE LARGE EGGS
CAYENNE TO TASTE
bLACK PEPPER
FINE ITALIAN bREAD CRUMbS
OIL FOR FRYING

SOAK FRESH COD IN WATER WITH TWO Tbs. OF COARSE SALT OVERNIGHT. PEEL AND CUT UP POTATOES. bOIL POTATOES AND ONIONS FOR 10-12 MINUTES AND THEN ADD DRAINED CODFISH. COOK UNTIL POTATOES ARE DONE. DRAIN WELL AND TRANSFER TO LARGE MIXING bOWL. MASH WITH A POTATO MASHER UNTIL WELL COMBINED. ADD PARSLEY. EGGS, CAYENNE, PEPPER. SHAPE INTO 2-3 INCH CAKES PUT bREAD CRUMbS IN A bOWL AND DIP CODFISH CAKES IN THE CRUMbS. FRY IN OIL UNTIL GOLDEN BROWN. SERVE WITH LEMON CAPER TARTAR SAUCE.

Lemon caper tartar Sauce

ONE CUP MAYONNAISE
HALF CUP SOUR CREAM
TWO Tbs. FRESH SQUEEZED
LEMON JUICE.
1/4 CUP EXTRA VIRGIN ♡ OLIVE OIL
ONE tsp. PREPARED DIJON
MUSTARD.
ONE Tbs. DRAINED CAPERS.
HALF CUP CHOPPED FLAT LEAF
PARSLEY
ONE tsp. MINCED GARLIC.

Findhorn
CAULIFLOWER
Cheese

BACK IN THE 1980's WHEN WE WERE BEGINNING TO GARDEN WITH THE ANGELS AND NATURE SPIRITS, THE STORY OF EILEEN CADDY, PETER CADDY AND DOROTHY MACLEAN AND THEIR GROUND BREAKING WORK AT FINDHORN IN NORTHERN SCOTLAND THRILLED AND INSPIRED US. HERE'S A RECIPE IN TRIBUTE TO THEM!!

ONE LARGE CAULIFLOWER, BROKEN INTO FLORETS AND STEAMED UNTIL NOT QUITE TENDER.

FOUR TBS. BUTTER
FOUR TBS. FLOUR
1/2 TSP. SALT
1/2 TSP. DRIED MUSTARD
TWO CUPS MILK OR
ONE CUP MILK AND ONE
CUP CAULIFLOWER COOKING
WATER.
TWO CUPS GRATED CHEDDAR
CHEESE
PAPRIKA.

PREHEAT OVEN TO 375°

MAKE CREAM SAUCE BY COOKING BUTTER, FLOUR AND MUSTARD TOGETHER FOR AT LEAST FIVE MINUTES ON LOW HEAT. SLOWLY ADD LIQUIDS. ADD CHEESE WHEN SAUCE IS THICKENED. PLACE CAULIFLOWER IN GREASED BAKING DISH AND POUR SAUCE OVER IT. BAKE FOR 30 MINUTES OR UNTIL SAUCE IS BUBBLY AND BROWNED ON TOP.

: GOAT CHEESE FRITTATA :

THIS RECIPE IS MORE A GENERAL TEMPLATE
THAN A HARD AND FAST LIST OF INGREDIENTS.
YOU CAN USE OTHER VEGETABLES THAN THE ONES
SUGGESTED, AND YOUR FRITTATA WILL BE DEL-
ICIOUS JUST THE SAME.

: ONE BUNCH SCALLIONS, CHOPPED : 2 Tbs
♡OLIVE OIL : 1 Tbs CHOPPED GARLIC : ½
CUP BASIL, CHOPPED : ONE 14oz CAN
ARTICHOKE HEARTS, DRAINED AND QUART-
ERED : ½ CUP KALAMATA ♡OLIVES, PITTED
AND SLICED IN HALF : ONE CUP CHERRY
TOMATOES, SLICED IN HALF : ½ tsp SEA
SALT : GROUND PEPPER TO TASTE : 8 LARGE
EGGS, BEATEN : FRESH GOAT CHEESE —
ONE CUP OR MORE :

IN AN OVEN PROOF FRY PAN LIKE A CAST-IRON PAN,
COOK SCALLIONS IN OIL ABOUT FIVE MINUTES THEN ADD
GARLIC AND COOK ANOTHER MINUTE. ADD BASIL, ARTICHOKE
HEARTS, ♡OLIVES, CHERRY TOMATOES, SALT AND PEPPER.

STIR GENTLY UNTIL EVERYTHING IS WARM THEN REDUCE
HEAT TO LOW AND POUR EGGS OVER INGREDIENTS.
COVER AND COOK UNTIL EGGS ARE FIRM ON BOTTOM,
ABOUT 5 MINUTES THEN PUT UNDER BROILER IN
OVEN AND BROIL UNTIL GOLDEN. SPRINKLE WITH
GOAT CHEESE AND BROIL ANOTHER MOMENT.
CUT AND SERVE.

FIVE MINUTE CHICKEN

WHILE THIS RECIPE DOES NOT COOK IN FIVE MINUTES IT CAN BE ASSEMBLED IN FIVE MINUTES BEFORE GOING IN THE OVEN.

JIM COOKED FOR HIMSELF DURING MOST OF HIS COLLEGE YEARS. WITH LIMITED TIME, MONEY AND SKILLS FOR THIS TASK, HE LEANED HEAVILY ON THIS DISH. IT WAS CERTAINLY BETTER THAN HIS ROOMMATES "TO GO" MEAL - TOMATO PASTE ON RAMEN, AND IN FACT, IS STILL SOMETHING WE HAVE FREQUENTLY.

ONE CUP UNCOOKED RICE

ONE CAN CREAM OF MUSHROOM OR CHICKEN SOUP.

ONE CAN WATER

½ CAN SHERRY

PINCH THYME

ONE CHOPPED UP ONION

ONE CUT UP CHICKEN OR CHICKEN PIECES OF YOUR CHOICE

SALT AND PEPPER

CAN OF ARTICHOKE HEARTS.

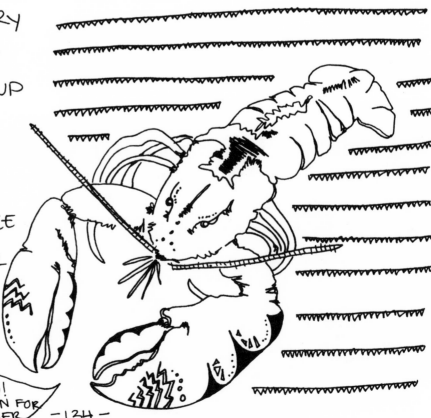

PHEW! CHICKEN FOR DINNER

PLACE ALL INGREDIENTS BUT
CHICKEN IN A SHALLOW BAKING
DISH LIKE A 9x13 INCH PAN.
USE FORK AND MIX TOGETHER.
PLACE CHICKEN ON TOP OF RICE
MIXTURE IN SINGLE LAYER.
COVER WITH FOIL AND BAKE FOR
ONE HOUR AT 350 DEGREES.
REMOVE FOIL AND ADD OPTIONAL
ARTICHOKE HEARTS AND BROIL
FOR 10-15 MINUTES UNTIL THE
CHICKEN IS BROWN.

grand DUKE'S Chicken

A FRIEND'S STINT COOKING IN A CHINESE RESTAURANT MEANT I GOT TO BENEFIT FROM WHAT SHE'D LEARNED. HERE'S HER TAKE TAKE ON GRAND DUKE'S CHICKEN.

1½ lb. BONELESS SKINLESS CHICKEN BREAST CUT IN ONE INCH CUBES.

1½ Tbs. SOY SAUCE

½ tsp. SUGAR

1 tsp. SESAME OIL

1 Tbs. RICE WINE OR DRY SHERRY.

ONE EGG WHITE

SCANT Tbs. CORNSTARCH

THREE LARGE GREEN PEPPERS, CUT IN ONE INCH PIECES.

TEN CLOVES GARLIC, MINCED FINELY

½ INCH PIECE FRESH GINGER, MINCED

FIVE SMALL DRIED RED PEPPERS, EACH CUT INTO FOUR PIECES (OR FEWER PEPPERS IF THIS IS TOO SPICY)

TWO SCALLIONS, GREEN AND WHITE PARTS CHOPPED CROSSWISE INTO ¼ INCH PIECES

ONE CUP SHELLED ROASTED PEANUTS

THANKS TO OUR SUPERVISORY CATS PENNY AND BELLA.

PUT CHICKEN IN A BOWL WITH SOY SAUCE, SUGAR, SESAME OIL, RICE WINE, EGG WHITE, CORNSTARCH AND SCALLIONS. SET ASIDE. HEAT TWO Tbs. PEANUT OIL IN WOK OR LARGE FRYING PAN OVER MEDIUM HIGH HEAT FOR 30 SECONDS THEN ADD GREEN PEPPER PIECES AND STIR FRY FOR 2-3 MINUTE. GREEN PEPPERS SHOULD STILL BE BRIGHT GREEN. REMOVE FROM PAN AND SET ASIDE.

ADD THREE Tbs OIL TO WOK AND HEAT FOR 30 SECONDS. ADD GARLIC, GINGER AND RED PEPPER AND STIR FOR 15 SECONDS. ADD CHICKEN AND ITS MARINADE. STIR FRY UNTIL COOKED 3-5 MINUTES (it WILL HAVE STIFFENED AND TURNED White.) ADD THE PEANUTS AND GREEN PEPPERS AND CONTINUE TO STIR FRY FOR 30 SECONDS MORE TO HEAT THOROUGHLY. SERVE WITH White RICE. IF THIS IS TOO SPICY FOR YOU, DECREASE THE NUMBER OF DRIED RED PEPPERS YOU USE.

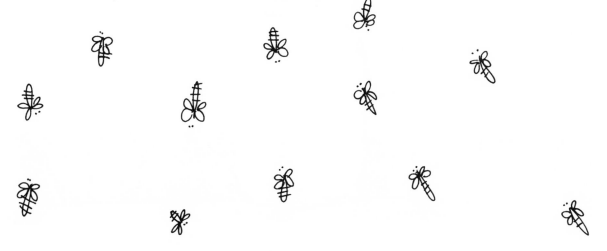

green ENCHILADAS

THIS IS ANOTHER RECIPE FROM OUR FRIEND EMILY CROMWELL.

TWO lbs. BONELESS CHICKEN BREAST
FOUR Tbs. UNSALTED BUTTER
ONE LARGE ONION
ONE lb. FRESH SPINACH
THREE CUPS SOUR CREAM (SOMETIMES WE MIX YOGURT WITH SOUR CREAM AND THE RECIPE ALSO WORKS WITH NO FAT SOUR CREAM)
TWO (4oz) CANS GREEN CHILIS DICED
ONE tsp. GROUND CUMIN
1/4 CUP MILK
12 FLOUR TORTILLAS
6oz. MONTEREY JACK CHEESE, SHREDDED.

POACH CHICKEN FOR 20 MINUTES THEN SHRED. SAUTE ONION IN BUTTER. STEAM SPINACH, RESERVE 1/2 CUP SPINACH WATER AND CHOP WHEN COOL. COMBINE ONIONS, SPINACH, SOUR CREAM, CHILIS, CUMIN, SPINACH LIQUID AND MILK.
THIS IS THE FILLING.

ADD HALF THE FILLING TO THE CHICKEN. PUT A GENEROUS AMOUNT OF THIS CHICKEN MIXTURE IN A LINE ON THE CENTER OF A TORTILLA THEN ROLL UP. REPEAT UNTIL ALL THE MIXTURE IS USED. LINE ROLLED TORTILLAS UP IN A BUTTERED 9x13" PAN. COVER FILLED TORTILLAS WITH HALF THE CHEESE, REMAINDER OF THE FILLING AND THEN REST OF THE CHEESE.
BAKE 30 MINUTES AT 350°.

LINGUINE WITH WHITE Clam SAUCE

WILL AND I GOT A BEE IN OUR BONNETS ABOUT FINDING
THE BEST WHITE CLAM SAUCE RECIPE WE COULD, AND
THIS IS THE RECIPE WE SETTLED ON AS THE WINNER.

THREE CLOVES GARLIC, MINCED
BIG PINCH RED PEPPER FLAKES
1/4 CUP ♡ OLIVE OIL
2-3 ANCHOVIES
3/4 CUP CLAM BROTH
TWO TBS. CHOPPED FRESH THYME
A GENEROUS HANDFUL OF FLAT LEAVED
   PARSLEY, CHOPPED
14 OUNCE CAN WHOLE BABY CLAMS, DRAINED
ONE lb. LINGUINE, COOKED UNTIL AL DENTE.
FRESH GROUND BLACK PEPPER TO TASTE.

HEAT GARLIC AND RED PEPPER FLAKES IN ♡ OLIVE
OIL UNTIL GARLIC SIZZLES THEN ADD ANCHOVIES.
STIR WITH A WOODEN SPOON UNTIL ANCHOVIES
MELT INTO OIL. BRING UP HEAT TO MEDIUM HIGH
ADD BROTH, THYME, PARSLEY AND PEPPER ALL AT
ONCE. ADD CLAMS. SHAKE PAN TO COMBINE
INGREDIENTS THEN ADD PASTA. TOSS THEN
TAKE OFF HEAT, LEAVING PASTA TO ABSORB
LIQUID. THIS FEEDS FOUR.

hungarian PORK GOULASH

3 lbs. LEAN BONELESS PORK CUT IN ONE INCH CUBES.

4 LARGE ONIONS SLICED THIN

3 Tbs PEANUT OIL

1 CLOVE GARLIC FINELY MINCED

1 Tbs. IMPORTED PAPRIKA.

SALT AND PEPPER TO TASTE.

½ tsp. MARJORAM.

BOILING CHICKEN BROTH.

1 lb. SAUERKRAUT

1 Tbs. CRUSHED CARAWAY SEEDS.

1 CUP SOUR CREAM.

HEAT HALF THE PEANUT OIL IN FRYING PAN. COOK THE ONIONS AND GARLIC UNTIL THEY START TO BROWN. STIR FREQUENTLY SO AS NOT TO BURN THE ONIONS. HEAT REMAINING OIL IN HEAVY OVEN PROOF CASSEROLE DISH AND COOK PORK UNTIL LIGHTLY BROWNED. ADD ONION AND GARLIC TO PORK.

ONE NEW YEAR'S EVE, I WALKED A BIG POT OF THIS GOULASH INTO A HUNGRY CROWD CAMPED OUT IN AN OUTING CLUB CABIN IN THE WHITE MOUNTAINS OF NEW HAMPSHIRE. AFTER CRASHING AROUND A SNOWY LANDSCAPE AT DUSK WITH AN ENORMOUS POT, IT OCCURRED TO ME THAT SIMPLER AND LIGHTER FARE MIGHT HAVE BEEN A WISER CHOICE ON MY PART. BUT IT WAS MUCH APPRECIATED BY ONE AND ALL, AND THE EMPTY POT WAS A LOT LIGHTER TO CARRY OUT THE NEXT DAY.

ADD SALT, PEPPER, MARJORAM AND PAPRIKA THEN POUR IN ENOUGH CHICKEN BROTH TO JUST BARELY COVER. BRING TO BOIL PARTLY COVERED, TURN-DOWN HEAT AND SIMMER FOR 30 MINUTES. ADD SAUERKRAUT AND CARAWAY SEEDS. COVER AND COOK AT 325 FOR ONE HOUR. TO SERVE, STIR IN SOUR CREAM. SERVE WITH BOILED OR ROASTED POTATOES. YOU CAN ALSO FREEZE THE GOULASH BEFORE THE ADDITION OF SOUR CREAM.

JIM'S FAMOUS 4 Cheese MACARONI

THREE Tbs. BUTTER
1/4 CUP FLOUR
THREE CUPS MILK
GENEROUS CHUNK OF GORGONZOLA CHEESE, CRUMBLED
CHUNK OF FONTINA CHEESE, GRATED OR CHEDDAR CHEESE
IF YOU DON'T WANT TO PAY FOR FONTINA.
PINCH OF NUTMEG
ONE Tsp. DRY MUSTARD
SALT AND PEPPER
ONE lb. ZITI, COOKED AL DENTE.
EIGHT oz. OF MOZZARELLA GRATED.
FOUR oz. OF PARMESAN GRATED.
ONE TSP PAPRIKA

JIM TEACHES SIXTH GRADE WHEN HE IS NOT KEEPING THE BOOKS OR BUILDING THE buildings FOR THE FARM. ONE YEAR FOR A SCHOOL FUND RAISER, JIM AND I COOKED THIS MACARONI AND CHEESE FOR THREE HUNDRED PEOPLE. SINCE THEN, JIM HAS BEEN EXPECTED TO BRING THIS TO ALL SCHOOL FUNCTIONS. FORTUNATELY HE LIKES MAKING IT, AND NO MATTER WHAT VARIATION OF CHEESES USED, IT ALWAYS LOOKS AND TASTES GREAT.

PREHEAT OVEN TO 350°. BUTTER BAKING DISH LIKE A 9x13" PAN. MELT BUTTER IN MEDIUM LARGE SAUCEPAN OVER MEDIUM HEAT. THEN ADD FLOUR, COOKING FOR A MINUTE OR TWO. GRADUALLY WHISK IN MILK. COOK STIRRING CONSTANTLY UNTIL SAUCE HAS THICKENED SLIGHTLY. THEN ADD GORGONZOLA AND FONTINA CHEESES AND STIR UNTIL THEY ARE MELTED. INTO THE SAUCE. ADD COOKED ZITI. STIR IN MOZZARELLA THEN POUR INTO BAKING PAN. SPRINKLE WITH PARMESAN AND THEN PAPRIKA. BAKE UNTIL BUBBLING AND GOLDEN BROWN ON TOP 30-40 MINUTES.

Kedgeree

THIS DISH DOES REQUIRE A FAIR NUMBER OF SAUCEPANS FOR ASSEMBLY, but it is delicious FOR BREAKFAST, LUNCH AND DINNER SO YOU WON'T HAVE TO MAKE ANYTHING ELSE FOR THE REST OF THE DAY.

FOUR EGGS

ONE CUP UNCOOKED BASMATI RICE
   OR THREE CUPS COOKED RICE.

1/2 lb SMOKED FISH (I USE SMOKED
   MACKEREL BECAUSE THAT IS WHAT
   I CAN FIND but SMOKED HADDOCK
   IS MORE TRADITIONAL.)

ONE CUP MILK.

ONE Tbs. butter

ONE MEDIUM ONION, CHOPPED FINE.

ONE CLOVE GARLIC CHOPPED FINE.

THREE Tbs. CURRY POWDER

ONE Tbs. FRESH LIME JUICE

HALF CUP CHOPPED FRESH CILANTRO
   LEAVES

1/4 CUP SLICED SCALLIONS.

SALT AND PEPPER TO TASTE.

PUT EGGS IN A SAUCEPAN AND COVER WITH COLD WATER, bring TO A SIMMER, COVER THE SAUCEPAN AND REMOVE FROM HEAT. LET EVERY-THING SIT FOR SIX MINUTES THEN RUN UNDER COLD WATER. PEEL, QUARTER AND SET ASIDE THE EGGS.

Cook rice the way you would cook a cup of rice. I usually use leftover rice when I make this dish. About 3 cups cooked rice works great. To get leftover rice, I make a double batch of basmati rice with cumin, use some of it immediately for a curry then use the rest the next day for the kedgeree.

Place smoked fish and milk in another saucepan and bring to a simmer. Cook until fish flakes easily, about five minutes. Remove from heat and flake. I use a boneless smoked fish but check for bones if yours might have any.

Melt butter in a large dutch oven type saucepan. Over medium heat. You are going to add everything to this pan. Add onions and garlic and cook until onions are soft, about five minutes. Add curry powder and then cook for another five minutes or so...

Add rice to curry and onions and mix well. Add haddock and milk and gently mix. Add lime juice, salt and pepper. Gently fold in eggs, scallions and cilantro. Retire from the kitchen for the day.
Your work is finished!

LAMB AND Eggplant PATITSIO

THE NICE THING ABOUT THIS DISH IS THAT THE MEAT LOVERS CAN EAT MORE OF THE bottom LAYER AND THE PASTA LOVERS CAN EAT MORE OF THE TOP LAYER.

FOR LAMB SAUCE:
ONE ONION, CHOPPED
ONE Tbs. ♡ OLIVE OIL
TWO lbs. LAMB STEW MEAT
ONE GARLIC CLOVE, MINCED
1 ½ tsp. SALT.
ONE tsp. DRIED OREGANO
½ tsp. CINNAMON
¼ tsp. bIack PEPPER.
ONE lb. EGGPLANT, PEELED AND CUT INTO 1" CUBES
ONE 28 to 32 oz CAN CRUSHED TOMATOES.

FOR CHEESE SAUCE:
TWO Tbs. UNSALTED butter
TWO Tbs. FLOUR
TWO CUPS MILK
½ lb. FETA (I USE MORE)
½ tsp. SALT.
¼ tsp. PEPPER
TWO LARGE EGGS.

FOR PASTA:
ONE bOX 16 oz PENNE.

MAKE LAMB SAUCE: SAUTÉ ONION, ADD LAMB ABOUT FIVE MINUTES UNTIL NO LONGER PINK. ADD GARLIC, OREGANO, SUGAR, CINNAMON, PEPPER AND SAUTÉ FOR A FEW MORE MINUTES. ADD TOMATOES AND EGGPLANT. GENTLY SIMMER, COVERED FOR 40 MINUTES. REMOVE lid AND SIMMER UNTIL SAUCE IS THICKENED. SEASON WITH SALT AND PEPPER.

MAKE CHEESE SAUCE: MELT BUTTER THEN STIR IN
FLOUR AND COOK, STIRRING, FOR TWO MINUTES.
WHISK IN MILK AND BRING TO A BOIL. REDUCE
HEAT AND SIMMER FOR FIVE MINUTES, ADD
FETA AND WHISK UNTIL WELL INCORPORATED.
ADD SALT AND PEPPER. BEAT EGGS IN BOWL.
ADD SOME OF THE SAUCE AND WHISK THEN
RETURN MIXTURE TO REST OF SAUCE AND
WHISK TOGETHER. COOK PASTA AND MIX WITH
CHEESE SAUCE.

PUT LAMB MIX IN BOTTOM OF WIDE SHALLOW
BAKING DISH - A 9x13" PAN WORKS WELL. PUT
PASTA AND CHEESE MIXTURE ON TOP. COOK
AT 425 UNTIL TOP IS GOLDEN 25-30 MINUTES.
LET STAND A FEW MINUTES BEFORE SERVING.

MEAT!

AND CHEESE PIE.

LIZ TAYLOR WORKED AT GREEN HOPE FARM UNTIL SHE LEFT TO RUN HER FAMILY'S SMOKE HOUSE. HER GREAT LOVE FOR ANIMALS INFUSED HER WORK HERE AND ALSO MEANT THAT SHE WENT HOME TO A FARM OF HORSES, COWS, DOGS AND CATS. THIS IS A RECIPE SHE SHARED FROM HER MOTHER'S SIDE OF THE FAMILY.

TWO lbs. LEAN GROUND BEEF ONE CUP FRESH BREAD CUBES TWO tsp. SALT HALF tsp. PEPPER TWO 10 oz PACKAGES FROZEN SPINACH, THAWED AND WELL DRAINED 16 oz SLICED PROVOLONE, CHOPPED ENOUGH PIE CRUST FOR FOUR PIE CRUSTS ONE EGG YOLK HALF lb. SLICED SALAMI, CHOPPED

COOK BEEF, DRAIN AND ADD SALT AND PEPPER AND BREAD CUBES. SET ASIDE! IN BOWL MIX SPINACH, CHEESE AND EGGS. SET ASIDE! TAKE 2/3 OF YOUR PIE CRUST DOUGH AND ROLL INTO A 16" CIRCLE ABOUT 1/8" THICK. FOLD IN FOURTHS AND CAREFULLY UNFOLD IN 10" SPRING FORM PAN. TRIM TO MAKE IT EVEN WITH TOP OF PAN. BRUSH BOTTOM OF PASTRY WITH EGG YOLK THEN SPOON IN BEEF MIXTURE. TOP WITH SPINACH CHEESE MIXTURE AND THEN SALAMI. FOLD EDGES OF PASTRY OVER FILLING. ROLL REMAINING PASTRY DOUGH INTO 10" ROUND AND PLACE OVER FILLING IN PAN. PRESS AROUND EDGES TO SEAL. COVER AND REFRIGERATE. ABOUT 1 1/2 HOURS BEFORE SERVING BRUSH TOP WITH EGG YOLK. BAKE ONE HOUR A 375°. COOL ON WIRE RACK FOR 10 MINUTES CAREFULLY REMOVE SPRING FORM RING. MAKES 10-12 SERVINGS.

MUSHROOM
···· bEAN ····
STROGANOFF

MY CHILDREN DID NOT LIKE THE ERA IN WHICH I COOKED ONLY VEGETARIAN. THEY CALL THESE THE "SEITAN YEARS". SOME VEGETARIAN RECIPES SURVIVED THE RETURN TO OMNIVOROUS EATING, AND THIS IS ONE OF THEM.

• • • • • • •

TEN OUNCES MUSHROOMS, SLICED.
ONE LARGE ONION, CHOPPED.
TWO MEDIUM CLOVES GARLIC, MINCED
1/4 CUP TAMARI
1/3 CUP SHERRY
1/2 tsp. ALLSPICE
1/2 tsp. MAJORAM OR BASIL
1/4 lb. buTTER
1/3 CUP FLOUR
ONE CUP SOUR CREAM
ONE CUP CHICK PEAS

• • • • • •

MELT BUTTER OVER VERY LOW HEAT, BEING CAREFUL NOT TO BROWN. ADD THE MUSHROOMS, ONIONS, GARLIC, SOY SAUCE, SHERRY, ALLSPICE, AND MAJORAM OR BASIL. COOK THE MIXTURE FOR 15-20 MINUTES OVER LOW HEAT UNTIL THE ONIONS ARE SOFT AND TRANSLUCENT. ADD FLOUR, STIRRING FREQUENTLY AND COOK 3-4 MINUTES MORE. ADD CHICK PEAS AND SOUR CREAM. SERVE OVER BROWN RICE OR NOODLES.

• •

⊳NEW MEXICO⊲
⊳POSOLE⊲

SINCE NONE OF US ARE FROM NEW MEXICO THIS IS PROBABLY NOT AUTHENTIC AT ALL, BUT WE LOVE IT ANYWAYS.

SAUTE PORK CHUNKS UNTIL BROWNISH AND ADD OTHER INGREDIENTS EXCEPT CHILI AND OREGANO. SIMMER FOR TWO HOURS THEN ADD REMAINING INGREDIENTS. COOK ABOUT half TO THREE FOURTHS OF AN HOUR. SERVE WITH FLOUR TORTILLAS AND HOT CHILI SAUCE IF DESIRED. WE AlSO SERVE WITH SHREDDED CHEESE.

▵ TWO lbs PORK SHOULDER OR LOIN CUT IN CHUNKS

▵ FOUR-FIVE CANS POSOLE (WHITE HOMINY)

▵ TWO CUPS WATER, PLUS.

▵ TWO ONIONS, CHOPPED

▵ THREE CLOVES GARLIC MINCED

▵ THREE tsp. Plus OR MINUS RED POWDERED CHILI OR TWO FRESH RED HOT CHILI PEPPERS.

▵ ONE Tbs OREGANO, CRUMBLED

▵ GENEROUS PINCH OF CUMIN AND ONE OF CORIANDER.

PASTA
alla
NORMA

This is a Sicilian recipe.

THREE GARLIC CLOVES
ONE lb. EGGPLANT, SMALL IF POSSIBLE
TWO LARGE CANS 28 OR 32oz WHOLE TOMATOES
ONE lb. RIDGED ZITI
1 1/4 CUP OLIVE OIL
3 oz OR MORE OF FRESHLY GRATED RICOTTA
SALATA CHEESE.

CUT EGGPLANT FIRST INTO HALF OR EVEN
QUARTERS IF LARGE AND THEN INTO 1/2 INCH
SLICES. FRY IN ♡LIVE OIL 'til GOLDEN BROWN.
DRAIN AND SEASON WITH SALT AND PEPPER.
DRAIN TOMATOES AND BREAK INTO PIECES.
SAUTE GARLIC IN SMALL AMOUNT OF ♡LIVE
OIL AND STIR IN TOMATOES. COOK FOR ABOUT
15 MINUTES. COOK PASTA THEN TOSS TOGETHER
GRATED RICOTTA SALATA, EGGPLANT PIECES,
TOMATO SAUCE AND ZITI. TOP WITH
MORE CHEESE.

It TAKES AWHILE TO FRY
THE EGGPLANT but
IT'S WORTH It.

PASTA PUTTANESCA

WE ACTUALLY CALL THIS "JIM'S PASTA" BECAUSE IT IS ONE OF HIS "GO TO" RECIPES WHEN HE IS COOKING SUPPER.

ONE lb. SPAGHETTI OR linguine

TWO CANS, TWO lbs. 3 oz EACH OF WHOLE TOMATOES, DRAINED WELL

1/4 CUP OLIVE OIL

ONE tsp. OREGANO, DRIED

1/2 tsp. DRIED RED PEPPER FLAKES

ONE CUP KALAMATA OLIVES, PITTED AND DRAINED

1/4 CUP CAPERS, DRAINED

4-8 GARLIC CLOVES CHOPPED

FLAT CAN OF ANCHOVIES, COARSELY CHOPPED

TWO Tsp. SALT

1/2 CUP PARSLEY COARSLEY CHOPPED.

COOK PASTA AT SAME TIME AS YOU MAKE THE Sauce.

TO MAKE SAUCE, COMBINE TOMATOES AND OLIVE OIL IN SKILLET AND BRING TO A BOIL. ADD REMAINING INGREDIENTS EXCEPT PASTA AND COOK FOR A FEW MINUTES UNTIL SAUCE HAS THICKENED TO YOUR LIKING. TOSS WITH COOKED PASTA AND SERVE.

ROASTED TOMATO BASIL PASTA

Sauce

Don't worry too much about amounts here. I never measure with this recipe, and the sauce is always wonderful.

Six lbs. fresh tomatoes, quartered.
One lb. onions coarsely chopped
Eight Tbs. ♡live oil
Thirty two cloves garlic, peeled
Two tsp. salt
One tsp pepper
Two cups chopped basil

Toss together everything but the basil and put on one or two rimmed cookie sheets depending on the volume you are working with. Bake uncovered at 450 degrees for at least 30-45 minutes or longer until skins are slightly brown. Turning the ingredients on the baking sheet occasionally will help.

The cooked mixture will not look great but after you have cooled the sauce, process in a food processor or blender until smooth. The sauce will then be a lovely almost deep pinkish red color.

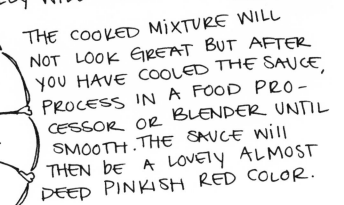

Stir in two cups chopped basil and you are set to go. This sauce also freezes well.

Ruth's Real Ohio Style Chili

This is a recipe from Jim's aunt Ruth who was a fabulous cook married to a lovely Cincinnati man named Tom Shively.

Tom, a master builder and electrical engineer, taught Jim how to do the electrical wiring for our farmhouse, and Tom also did all the complicated electrical work like tying all the wires into the main electrical box.

The box remains a thing of beauty, and we remain deeply grateful for Tom's impeccable work and his wife's impeccable recipes.

Three lbs. ground chuck
One 46 ounce can tomato juice or equivalent in tomato sauce (the traditional choice is juice)
Three Tbs. dried onion flakes.
Two rounded tsp garlic powder.
One rounded Tbs. salt
One rounded Tbs. chili powder.
One rounded tsp cumin
One rounded tsp paprika
Half tsp. thyme.
Half tsp level red pepper

Half tsp. majoram
Half tsp. oregano
Half tsp. cinnamon
1/4 tsp. allspice
12 cloves
15 small bay leaves
1/4 tsp rosemary needles
5 whole hot red cherry peppers.

BROWN MEAT. ADD REST OF INGREDIENTS AND
A QUART OF WATER. RETAIN THIS CONSISTENCY
DURING COOKING PROCESS AND COOK THREE
HOURS, UNCOVERED. STIR OFTEN TO MIX SPICES.
CLOVES, BAY LEAVES AND ROSEMARY CAN BE
PUT IN tea STRAINER FOR EASY REMOVAL AT
END OF COOKING TIME. SERVE OVER
SPAGHETTI WITH AMERICAN CHEESE FOR A
TRADITIONAL OHIO MEAL.

ROSEMARY
GOAT CHEESE
AND
Chicken
MACARONI AND CHEESE

THIS VARIATION OF MACARONI AND
CHEESE HAS BEEN WILDLY POPULAR
IN OUR HOUSEHOLD, PERHAPS EXPLAIN-
ING WHY I HAVE SO MANY ROSE-
MARY PLANTS IN THE GREENHOUSE.

ONE lb. PASTA - SHAPE OF YOUR CHOICE
ONE QUART HALF AND HALF
TWO Tbs. FRESH ROSEMARY, CHOPPED FINE
TWO CUPS ROAST CHICKEN, LEFTOVERS
    FROM ANOTHER MEAL WORK GREAT
    HERE.
EIGHT OUNCES GOAT CHEESE

Salt AND *pepper*

PUT CREAM IN POT WITH ROSEMARY
AND A PINCH OF SALT AND SIMMER
UNTIL REDUCED BY HALF. ADD
CHICKEN AND SIMMER ANOTHER
30 MINUTES UNTIL SAUCE
COATS BACK OF A SPOON.
COOK PASTA ACCORDING
TO PACKAGE DIRECTIONS
AND ADD TO SAUCE ALONG
WITH THE GOAT CHEESE.
TOSS AND SERVE.

Shrimp Curry
FROM GOA

HALF tsp. CAYENNE
ONE Tbs. PAPRIKA
HALF tsp. TURMERIC
FOUR GARLIC CLOVES
(PEELED AND CRUSHED)
ONE INCH PIECE GINGER,
(PEELED AND GRATED)
TWO Tbs. CORIANDER
        SEEDS.
ONE tsp. CUMIN SEEDS
ONE 14 oz. CAN OF
COCONUT MILK, WELL
        STIRRED
3/4 tsp. SALT (OR TO TASTE)
ONE Tbs. TAMARIND PASTE
(THIS CAN BE FOUND WITH
OTHER THAI INGREDIENTS IN
A LOT OF SUPERMARKETS—
THE RECIPE WORKS FINE
WITHOUT IT IF YOU CAN'T
FIND IT.)
ONE lb. MEDIUM UNCOOKED
SHRIMP, DEVEINED.

MIX CAYENNE, PAPRIKA, TURMERIC
GARLIC AND GINGER WITH 1 1/4
CUP WATER. MIX WELL. GRIND
CORIANDER AND CUMIN SEEDS
IN A COFFEE GRINDER OR BLEND-
ER AND ADD TO MIXTURE. PUT
THIS LIQUID IN A COOKING PAN
AND BRING TO A SIMMER. TURN
HEAT TO MEDIUM LOW AND
SIMMER FOR TEN MINUTES. THE
SAUCE SHOULD REDUCE AND
THICKEN. ADD COCONUT MILK,
SALT, TAMARIND PASTE AND
BRING TO SIMMER. ADD SHRIMP
AND SIMMER UNTIL OPAQUE
AND JUST COOKED THROUGH.
        SERVES FOUR.

Spaghetti Sauce

MADE FAMOUS BY
MEL SHEEHAN.

JIM'S DAD LOVED HIS TOMATO PLANTS AND
VISITED WITH THEM EVERY DAY. WHEN I FIRST
MARRIED JIM HIS FAMILY WOULD OFTEN
ARRIVE FOR A VISIT WITH A CASE OF THIS
SAUCE, MADE WITH TOMATOES LOVINGLY
GROWN, HARVESTED, COOKED AND CANNED
BY MEL.
MEL WAS NOT A NICKNAME FOR MELVIN BUT
A NICKNAME FOR MELON HEAD. JIM AND HIS
DAD GREW UP ON JAMESTOWN, Rhode ISLAND,
A SMALL ISLAND IN NARRAGANSETT BAY
WHERE EVERYONE HAD AN UNUSUAL NICK-
NAME. JIM'S DAD GOT HIS BECAUSE HE
WAS BORN WITH A VERY
LARGE HEAD.

3½ CUPS CHOPPED ONIONS

ONE GREEN PEPPER, DICED

4-5 CELERY STALKS WHOLE

20 CUPS RAW TOMATOES,
BLENDERIZED WITH
SKINS.

1 Tbs. PEPPER

1 Tbs. OREGANO

½ CUP SUGAR

1 Tbs. GARLIC POWDER

3 Tbs. SALT

5-6 BAY LEAVES

8 SMALL CANS TOMATO
PASTE.

MEL USED A CUP OF SUGAR but I USE
½ CUP SUGAR. THIS WILL NEED TO COOK
FOR TWO HOURS. THEN YOU REMOVE
THE CELERY AND BAY LEAVES AND ADD
EIGHT SMALL CANS OF TOMATO PASTE
COOK 30 MINUTES MORE.

Stuffed GRAPE Leaves

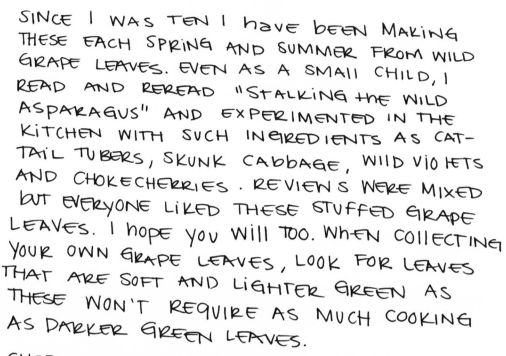

SINCE I WAS TEN I have BEEN MAKING THESE EACH SPRING AND SUMMER FROM WILD GRAPE LEAVES. EVEN AS A SMALL CHILD, I READ AND REREAD "STALKING THE WILD ASPARAGUS" AND EXPERIMENTED IN THE KITCHEN WITH SUCH INGREDIENTS AS CAT-TAIL TUBERS, SKUNK CABBAGE, WILD VIOLETS AND CHOKECHERRIES. REVIEWS WERE MIXED BUT EVERYONE LIKED THESE STUFFED GRAPE LEAVES. I hope YOU WILL TOO. WHEN COLLECTING YOUR OWN GRAPE LEAVES, LOOK FOR LEAVES THAT ARE SOFT AND LIGHTER GREEN AS THESE WON'T REQUIRE AS MUCH COOKING AS DARKER GREEN LEAVES.

TWO CHOPPED ONIONS, 1 lb. GROUND BEEF OR LAMB, 3 Tbs. butter, ½ CUP UNCOOKED RICE, 30-50 GRAPE LEAVES DEPENDING ON SIZE, TWO OR MORE CUPS OF WATER, 2 tsp SALT, ¼ tsp PEPPER

SAUTE ONIONS AND MEAT IN butter. REMOVE FROM HEAT AND MIX IN RICE. PLACE MIXTURE ON LEAVES, A SPOON-FUL OR TWO FOR EACH LEAF. Wrap UP LIKE AN ENVELOPE AND PLACE STUFFED LEAVES SIDE by SIDE IN A LARGE FLAT SAUCEPAN THAT CAN be PUT ON THE STOVETOP. ADD WATER, SALT AND PEPPER. SIMMER FOR 30-40 MINUTES SPOONING WATER OVER LEAVES OCCASIONALLY ADD MORE WATER IF NECESSARY TO KEEP LEAVES JUST BARELY COVERED. SERVE WITH EGG LEMON SAUCE.

Egg Lemon Sauce

3 EGGS
1 tsp. CORN STARCH
    A LITTLE COLD WATER
JUICE OF ONE LEMON
    SALT AND PEPPER to TASTE
STOCK FROM GRAPE LEAVES

BEAT EGGS. ADD CORN STARCH DILUTED WITH
A LITTLE BIT OF COLD WATER. ADD LEMON
JUICE, SALT AND PEPPER. GRADUALLY ADD
MEAT STOCK DRAINED FROM THE SAUCEPAN
WHERE YOU HAVE BEEN COOKING THE STUFFED
LEAVES. WHEN EGG AND LEMON SAUCE IS WELL
MIXED WITH THE STOCK, RETURN TO SAUCE-
PAN CONTAINING GRAPE LEAVES AND COOK
UNTIL SAUCE IS SLIGHTLY THICKENED.

SUMMER
SQUASH
Stuffed
PEPPERS

LAURA'S FIRST YEAR HERE, SHE WAS SET TO WORK DESIGNING, PLANTING AND MAINTAINING THE MAIN VEGETABLE GARDEN AT THE FARM. SUMMER SQUASH AND PEPPERS WERE KEY PLAYERS IN HER BEAUTIFUL DESIGN, SO THE RECIPE FOR THIS BEAUTIFUL AND DELICIOUS DISH CAME IN HANDY. TASTE TESTERS AT THE FARM LOVED THIS MADE WITH SUMMER SQUASH, BUT LAURA SAYS IT IS EQUALLY GOOD WITH ANY VEGETABLES FROM THE GARDEN. ◉ ◉ ◉ ◉ ◉ ◉ ◉ ◉

TWO GREEN OR RED bell PEPPERS, CUT IN HALF AND CLEANED ◤◥ TWO CUPS SUMMER SQUASH, CUT IN SMALL PIECES ◤◥ ONE CUP black BEANS ◤◥ THREE CUPS COOKED RICE (ONE CUP UNCOOKED RICE) ◤◥ ONE ONION, CHOPPED ◤◥ TWO CLOVES GARLIC, MINCED ◤◥ ONE CUP GRATED CHEDDAR CHEESE OR MORE IF YOU PREFER ◤◥ ¾ CUP ENCHILADA SAUCE ◤◥ SALT ◤◥ ONE tsp. GROUND CUMIN ◤◥ PINCH CRUSHED RED PEPPER ◤◥ 1 OR 2 Tbs. ♡OLIVE OIL ◤◥

◉ ◉ ◉ ◉ ◉

ADD TO THE COOKED RICE THE GROUND CUMIN AND CRUSHED RED PEPPER AND PUT IN THE BOTTOM OF A GREASED BAKING DISH. IN A FRY PAN, SAUTE ONION, GARLIC AND SUMMER SQUASH IN OIL UNTIL TENDER THEN ADD BLACK BEANS. PLACE PEPPER HALVES FACE DOWN ON A BAKING DISH AND BROIL IN THE OVEN FOR 5-10 MINUTES. TAKE THESE BROILED PEPPER HALVES AND PUT RIGHT SIDE UP NESTLED IN THE RICE. INTO EACH PEPPER SCOOP THE SAUTEED VEGETABLES AND BLACK BEANS. IF IT ALL DOESN'T FIT INSIDE THE PEPPERS, PUT THE REST ON TOP OF THE RICE. POUR ENCHILADA SAUCE OVER EVERYTHING AND THEN TOP WITH GRATED CHEESE. BAKE AT 350 DEGREES FOR 20-30 MINUTES. ◎ ◎ ◎ ◎ ◎

SWEET AND SOUR MEATBALLS IN ACORN SQUASH

THIS IS A DISH I MADE A LOT WHEN THE KIDS WERE little. When collecting recipes for this cookbook, the recipe resurfaced AND HAS JOINED THE KITCHEN REPERTOIRE ONCE AGAIN.

3 ACORN SQUASH, CUT IN HALF

1 lb. SAUSAGE, MILD Italian WORKS well

½ lb. GROUND BEEF

1 CLOVE GARLIC, MINCED

3/4 CUP SOFT bread CRUMbs

1 EGG

1 tsp. GROUND GINGER

1 Tbs. PARSLEY, CHOPPED

8 oz CAN PINEAPPLE CHUNKS.

1 TBS. SOY SAUCE

1 TBS. brown SUGAR

½ CUP beef broth

½ CUP CATSUP

½ tsp. MUSTARD

½ CUP CHOPPED GREEN PEPPERS.

PREHEAT OVEN TO 350 DEGREES.

CUT SQUASH IN HALF, DIG OUT SEEDS AND PLACE CUT SIDE DOWN IN A 9 X 13" PAN WITH AN INCH OF WATER. BAKE 45 MINUTES OR UNTIL SQUASH CAN BE EASILY PIERCED WITH FORK. MEANWHILE, COMBINE SAUSAGE, GROUND BEEF, GARLIC, bread CRUMBS, EGG, 1/2 tsp GINGER AND PARSLEY. MIX WELL AND FORM INTO ONE INCH balls. bake MEATballs ON A COOKIE SHEET FOR 15 MINUTES AT 350 DEGREES.

TO MAKE SAUCE, DRAIN JUICE FROM THE PINEAPPLE INTO SAUCEPAN THEN ADD SOY SAUCE, brown SUGAR, broth, CATSUP, 1/2 tsp GINGER AND MUSTARD. COOK 15 MINUTES, STIRRING. THEN ADD PINEAPPLE CHUNKS, GREEN PEPPERS AND MEATballs TO THE SAUCE. PUT MEATball MIXTURE INTO SQUASH AND WARM bRiEFLY IN THE OVEN. SERVE WITH RICE.

THIS IS AMBER. A LOVABLE, SWEET HORSE ACROSS THE STREET FROM THE FARM. WE FEED HER APPLES AT LUNCH.

SPINACH PIE with MUENSTER crust

THIS RECIPE IS MUCH BETTER THAN IT SOUNDS. THE MUENSTER MAKES AN AMAZINGLY GOOD CRUST. VARIOUS PEOPLE AROUND HERE HAVE BEEN KNOWN TO FIGHT OVER WHO GETS THE LEFTOVERS FOR LUNCH THE NEXT DAY. I NOW MAKE TWO PIES AT THE SAME TIME TO SOLVE THIS PROBLEM.

LINE TEN INCH PIE PAN WITH OVER-LAPPING SLICES OF MUENSTER CHEESE. COVER BOTTOM OF PAN AND SIDES. COMBINE COOKED AND DRAINED SPINACH WITH COTTAGE CHEESE, EGGS, ONIONS, PARMESAN DILL, AND PEPPER. POUR IN PIE PLATE AND COOK AT 350 DEGREES FOR ONE HOUR. ALLOW TO STAND FIVE MINUTES BEFORE SLICING.

THIS CAN ALSO BE EATEN COLD OR REHEATED.

1 lb. SLICED MUENSTER CHEESE

THREE 10 oz. PACKAGES FROZEN SPINACH, COOKED AND DRAINED WELL.

ONE CUP COTTAGE CHEESE

3 EGGS, BEATEN

ONE SMALL ONION, CHOPPED.

1/3 CUP GRATED PARMESAN CHEESE OR TO TASTE.

ONE TSP. DRIED DILL

SALT AND PEPPER TO TASTE.

WHAT A HAPPY TIME OF THE YEAR WHEN THE BASIL IS ABUND- ANT IN THE GARDENS AND TOMATOES TOO!!

FOUR RIPE TOMATOES CUT
   IN PIECES
ONE lb. bRIE CHEESE WITH
   RIND REMOVED CUT IN
   IRREGULAR PIECES.
ONE CUP BASIL LEAVES,
   CUT IN STRIPS
THREE GARLIC CLOVES,
   PEELED AND MINCED
ONE CUP BEST QUALITY
   OLIVE OIL
HALF tsp. SALT
   HALF tsp. GROUND
      PEPPER.
1½ lb. LINGUINE
PARMESAN CHEESE.

COMBINE TOMATOES, BRIE, BASIL, GARLIC, OLIVE OIL, SALT AND PEPPER. LEAVE IN A BOWL AT ROOM TEMP- ERATURE FOR AT LEAST 2 HOURS.

COOK PASTA IN WELL-SALTED WATER. DRAIN AND TOSS WITH SAUCE. TOP EACH SERVING WITH PARMESAN CHEESE.

TOMATOES, BRIE AND BASIL
Linguine

TOMATO PIE

JIM HAS THE BEST HAND AT
PASTRY IN THE FAMILY, AND
SO HE MAKES THE TOMATO
PIES, USUALLY TWO AT A TIME

BLEND: TWO CUPS
FLOUR, ONE STICK
BUTTER, FOUR tsp
BAKING POWDER, AND
ABOUT 3/4 CUP MILK

ROLL OUT HALF THE DOUGH ON A FLOURED
SURFACE AND LINE A 9" PIE PAN WITH
THE DOUGH.

USE EITHER 2 lbs. PEELED FRESH TOMATOES
OR TWO 28 oz CANS OF GOOD CANNED
TOMATOES. DRAIN WELL. SLICE OVER CRUST
AND TOP WITH CHIVES, BASIL, SCALLIONS
WHATEVER YOU FEEL LIKE. GRATE AT
LEAST 1½ CUP SHARP CHEDDAR· AND
SPRINKLE ABOUT 2/3 OF IT ON THE TOM-
ATOES. DRIZZLE 1/3 CUP MAYONNAISE
THAT HAS BEEN THINNED WITH 2 Tbs.
OF LEMON JUICE OVER THE CHEESE
AND THEN ADD THE REST OF THE
CHEESE. ROLL OUT REMAINING DOUGH.
FIT OVER FILLING, PINCH TOGETHER
AND CUT STEAM VENTS. BAKE THE
PIE FOR 25 MINUTES AT 400 DEGREES.
THIS PIE TASTES BEST IF COOLED AND
THEN REHEATED AT 350 DEGREES
UNTIL IT IS HOT.

THE PROPORTIONS DON'T
SEEM TO MATTER
SO USE MORE OR LESS
TOMATOES, CHEESE,
AND HERBS.

WILL'S FAVORITE PASTA WITH HOT ITALIAN
SAUSAGE:
WE GROW OVATION SPICY GREENS FROM JOHNNY'S SELECTED SEEDS AND USE THEM IN THIS DISH. WHEN THEY BOLT LATER IN THE GROWING SEASON I USE SWISS CHARD. IN BOTH CASES I CHOP THE GREENS.

ONE MEDIUM ONION, CHOPPED
TWO Tbs. ♡OLIVE OIL
TWO lbs. HOT ITALIAN SAUSAGE
ONE lb. PASTA, YOUR CHOICE OF SHAPE
BUNCH OF SWISS CHARD OR MIXED
SPICY GREENS, CHOPPED FINE
PARMESAN CHEESE

SAUTE CHOPPED ONION IN ♡OLIVE OIL IN HEAVY BOTTOMED DUTCH OVEN TYPE POT. REMOVE SAUSAGE FROM CASINGS AND ADD TO ONIONS. BREAK UP SAUSAGE AS IT COOKS. WHEN SAUSAGE IS COOKED, STIR IN SWISS CHARD OR GREENS, TURN OFF HEAT AND COVER POT.

IN SEPARATE POT, COOK PASTA. WHEN COOKED, DRAIN BUT KEEP ABOUT HALF A CUP OF THE PASTA WATER. ADD PASTA AND RESERVED PASTA WATER TO SAUSAGE MIX AND STIR WELL. SERVE WITH PARMESAN CHEESE.

VEGETARIAN Shepherd's Pie

THIS IS A WONDERFUL MEAT FREE VERSION OF shepherd's pie. EVEN THE CHILDREN WHO OFTEN HATED THE FOOD DURING MY VEGETARIAN YEARS, LIKED THIS RECIPE.

My brief stint at hard core vegetarianism happened in the 1980's. To this day the children collectively refer to these years as the Seitan years and celebrate that they are behind us.

FOR THE FILLING:
ONE Tbs. OIL
HALF CUP CHOPPED ONIONS
HALF lb. MUSHROOMS, SLICED
1 1/2 CUPS COTTAGE CHEESE,
        DRY CURD PREFERABLY
ONE EGG, LIGHTLY BEATEN
1/4 tsp. PEPPER SAUCE
ONE tsp. POULTRY SEASONING
OR GENEROUS PINCH EACH OF
GROUND SAGE, GROUND THYME,
AND GROUND MARJORAM
1 1/2 tsp. SOY SAUCE

TOPPING:
SEVERAL CUPS OF MASHED POTATOES
ONE Tbs. BUTTER
PAPRIKA.

SAUTE ONION IN OIL FOR A FEW MINUTES. ADD MUSHROOMS AND SAUTE UNTIL JUST TENDER. REMOVE FROM HEAT AND MIX WITH COTTAGE CHEESE, EGG AND SEASONINGS. PLACE IN DEEP 9 INCH PAN OR TWO QUART BAKING DISH. COVER WITH MASHED POTATOES, DOT WITH BUTTER AND SPRINKLE WITH PAPRIKA. BAKE AT 350° FOR 30 MINUTES UNTIL POTATOES ARE LIGHTLY COLORED.

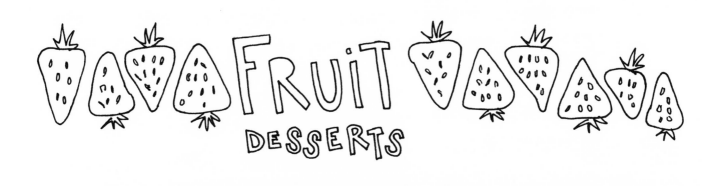

Fruit
DESSERTS

apple CRISP
CROSTATA

MANY KINDS OF APPLES WILL WORK PERFECTLY WITH THIS RECIPE. WE USE WHATEVER IS RIPE AND READY FROM OUR APPLE TREES. OUR FAVORITE APPLE TREE IS AN ESOPUS SPITZENBERG BUT WE HAVE MANY OTHER TREES WITH INTERESTING NAMES AND FLAVORS INCLUDING A WINTER BANANA, A WOLF RIVER, A BALDWIN AND A GRAVENSTEIN.

CRUST: 2 1/4 CUPS FLOUR : 1/2 tsp. SALT : 3/4 CUP BUTTER : 1/4 CUP VEGETABLE SHORTENING : 1/4 CUP ICE WATER :

BLEND DRY INGREDIENTS EITHER IN FOOD PROCESSOR WITH A FEW SHORT PULSES OR BY HAND ADD ICE COLD WATER SLOWLY UNTIL DOUGH JUST HOLDS TOGETHER. WRAP IN PLASTIC AND REFRIGERATE FOR AN HOUR. ROLL OUT IN BIG PIECE. I ROLL IT ON A COOKIE SHEET WITH A PIECE OF PARCHMENT PAPER UNDER IT BEFORE PUTTING THE APPLE FILLING ON IT AND FINALLY TURNING UP THE SIDES OF DOUGH SO THAT JUICES FROM THE APPLES WILL NOT RUN OUT DURING COOKING.

APPLE CRISP FILLING AND TOPPING

12 APPLES
TWO CUPS SUGAR, BROWN OR WHITE.
HALF tsp. GROUND CLOVES.
HALF tsp. CINNAMON.
FOUR tsp. LEMON JUICE
1 1/2 CUP FLOUR
PINCH SALT
12 Tbs. butter.

PEEL, CORE AND SLICE APPLES INTO A BOWL. ADD HALF THE SUGAR AND THE SPICES AND LEMON JUICE. MIX LIGHTLY AND PUT ON ROLLED OUT CRUST AND AS SAID PREVIOUSLY BEND THE DOUGH UP ONTO THE APPLES TO SEAL IN JUICES. THE IRREGULAR EDGES OF THE CRUST ON THE APPLES LOOK VERY ELEGANT ANYWAYS.

Blend REMAINING SUGAR, butter, FLOUR AND SALT TOGETHER UNTIL MIXTURE HAS A CRUMBLY CONSISTENCY. SPRINKLE ON APPLE FILLING. COOK AT 350 FOR ABOUT AN HOUR. CAN BE SERVED WITH VANILLA ICE CREAM (can't EVERYTHING?).

apple MAPLE CUSTARD PIE

WE MAKE THIS PIE WITH LOTS OF DIFFERENT KINDS OF APPLES. I DON'T THINK RED DELICIOUS HAVE MUCH FLAVOR SO THAT IS WHY I INCLUDED THE CAVEAT NOT TO USE THIS VARIETY. YOU CAN ALSO MAKE THIS DESSERT WITH A HALF CUP OF HONEY INSTEAD OF THE MAPLE SYRUP IF YOU PREFER.

PREHEAT OVEN TO 375° SPREAD SLICED APPLES IN PIE SHELL. COMBINE THE REST OF THE INGREDIENTS IN A BLENDER AND RUN AT HIGH SPEED FOR SEVERAL SECONDS. A WHISK OR ROTARY EGG BEATER WILL ALSO WORK FINE. POUR IN PIE SHELL OVER APPLES AND BAKE FOR 45 MINUTES OR UNTIL SOLID WHEN JIGGLED. COOL TO ROOM TEMPERATURE BEFORE SLICING.

ONE 9" PIE SHELL, UNBAKED
TWO CUPS PEELED AND THINLY SLICED APPLES (ANY VARIETY BUT RED DELICIOUS)
FOUR EGGS
3/4 CUP MAPLE SYRUP
ONE CUP PLAIN YOGURT, (WHOLE MILK WORKS BEST)
ONE tsp. VANILLA
1/2 tsp CINNAMON
PINCH OF SALT.

APPLE TART a la TEDDY

DEAR FRIEND AND COOKING MENTOR, TEDDY GROBE, ALWAYS ELEVATED HER PIES AND TARTS by PUTTING ALMOND PASTE ON THE BOTTOM CRUST UNDER THE FRUIT. SINCE ALMOND PASTE IS VERY HARD, I FIND IT EASIEST TO GRATE IT ONTO THE CRUST WITH A BOX GRATER.

1¼ CUP FLOUR

FOUR Tbs. SUGAR

ONE STICK butter, (CUT IN PIECES)

TWO EGG YOLKS

PINCH OF SALT

GRATED RIND OF ONE LEMON

TUBE OF ALMOND PASTE

APPLES, PEELED, CORED AND SLICE THINLY

12 OUNCES APriCOT PRESERVES

WHIPPING CREAM.

PREHEAT OVEN TO A HOT 425 DEGREES. SIFT THE FLOUR ONTO THE COUNTER OR PASTRY bOARD MAKE A WELL IN THE CENTER AND ADD THE SUGAR, butter, EGG YOLKS, SALT AND LEMON RIND. MAKE THESE INGREDIENTS INTO A PASTE THEN KNEAD INTO FLOUR. REFRIGERATE FOR HALF AN HOUR OR MORE WRAPPED IN PARCHMENT PAPER. ROll OUT TO A LARGE DISK AND TRANSFER TO 9 OR 10" TART SHELL. COVER DOUGH WITH THE ALMOND PASTE.

PLACE APPLES IN A SPIRAL, STARTING IN THE CENTER THEN FANNING OUT TO THE OUTSIDE EDGES. SPREAD WITH APRICOT PRESERVES. HEATING THE PRESERVES IN A SMALL SAUCEPAN WILL MAKE THEM EASIER TO SPREAD. BAKE AT 425° FOR 15 MINUTES THEN REDUCE OVEN TO 35° DEGREES AND BAKE. FOR 30 MINUTES LONGER. SPRINKLE WITH CONFECTIONER'S SUGAR.

Apple WALNUT Cake

THIS IS OUR FAVORITE APPLE DESSERT. WE OUGHT TO GET TIRED OF IT, but WE JUST DON'T. IT IS WORTH GETTING A bottle OF CALVADOS JUST TO HAVE FOR THIS RECIPE. REALLY.

1½ CUP VEGETABLE OIL
2 CUPS SUGAR
3 EGGS
3 CUPS FLOUR

PINCH OF GROUND CLOVES
1 tsp BAKING SODA
1½ tsp CINNAMON
½ tsp FRESHLY GRATED NUTMEG
½ tsp SALT
1¼ CUPS WALNUTS, COARSELY CHOPPED
4 CUPS CHUNKS OF PEELED AND CORED GOOD COOKING APPLES OF YOUR CHOICE.
3 Tbs. CALVADOS

APPLE CIDER GLAZE.

4 Tbs butter
8 Tbs BROWN SUGAR
3 Tbs CALVADOS
6 Tbs CIDER
2 Tbs CREAM!

TO MAKE THE GLAZE, MELT BUTTER AND SUGAR TOGETHER THEN ADD REMAINING INGREDIENTS. BRING TO A BOIL THEN REDUCE HEAT SLIGHTLY AND COOK FOR FIVE MINUTES.

FOR CAKE, PREHEAT OVEN TO 325°. IN LARGE BOWL BEAT VEGETABLE OIL AND SUGAR UNTIL THICK AND OPAQUE. ADD EGGS ONE AT A TIME, BEATING WELL AFTER EACH ADDITION. SIFT DRY INGREDIENTS THEN ADD TO OIL AND EGG MIXTURE AND MIX WELL. ADD WALNUTS, APPLES AND CALVADOS ALL TOGETHER AND STIR UNTIL MIXED. POUR BATTER INTO GREASED ANGEL FOOD TIN. BAKE FOR ONE HOUR AND FIFTEEN MINUTES OR UNTIL CAKE TESTER COMES OUT CLEAN. LET CAKE REST TEN MINUTES THEN UNMOLD AND POUR GLAZE OVER TOP.

Baked Pears

IN AMONGST OUR APPLE TREES ARE
A NUMBER OF WONDERFUL PEAR TREES.
PEARS MUST BE PICKED BEFORE THEY
RIPEN ON THE TREE TO AVOID MUSHY
FRUIT. THIS MEANS LATE IN THE
SUMMER WE OFTEN HAVE A WHEEL-
BARROW AT THE BACK DOOR LADEN
WITH RIPENING PEARS. IN BETWEEN
EATING THE PEARS RIGHT OUT OF THE
WHEEL BARROW OR CANNING THEM UP,
WE ALSO MAKE THIS SIMPLE BUT
DELICIOUS DESSERT.

- SIX FIRM PEARS
- THREE FOURTHS CUP CONFECTIONER'S SUGAR
- THREE tbs. BUTTER
- HALF CUP HEAVY cream.

PEEL AND QUARTER THE PEARS.
ARRANGE IN BAKING DISH.
SPRINKLE WITH SUGAR AND
DOT WITH BUTTER. BAKE at
FOUR HUNDRED DEGREES FOR
FORTY MINUTES OR UNTIL
TENDER AND SUGAR IS DARK
BROWN. BASTE FREQUENTLY
ADD hot CREAM. BAKE
TEN MINUTES LONGER AND
SERVE WARM.

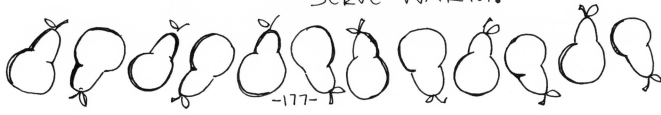

BLITZ TORTE with STAWBERRIES and cream

THIS IS A BEAUTIFUL DESSERT AND A FREQUENT CELEBRATION DESSERT FROM MY CHILDHOOD.

PREHEAT OVEN TO 325 DEGREES.

1½ CUP SUGAR (½ CUP USED IN CAKE, 1 CUP
   USED IN COOKED MERINGUE)
¼ CUP butter
   4 EGG YOLKS
½ tsp. VANILLA THEN 1 tsp. VANILLA
   FOR MERINGUE
7/8 OF A CUP OF REGULAR FLOUR
   OR 1 CUP CAKE FLOUR
1 tsp. BAKING POWDER
   ¼ tsp SALT
   5 Tbs. CREAM
   4 EGG WhiteS

BEAT butter UNTIL SOFT AND ADD ½ CUP SUGAR. BLEND UNTIL LIGHT AND CREAMY THEN ADD 4 EGG YOLKS, ONE AT A TIME. ADD ½ tsp VANILLA. SIFT FLOUR WITH BAKING POWDER AND SALT THEN ADD TO batter ALTERNATING WITH CREAM. BEAT UNTIL SMOOTH AND THEN SPREAD IN TWO GREASED 9 INCH CAKE PANS. WHip EGG WhiteS UNTIL STIFF but NOT DRY THEN ADD THE REMAINING CUP OF SUGAR SLOWly, ABOUT A Tbs. AT A TIME. BEAT CONSTANTly. WHEN ALL THE SUGAR HAS BEEN ADDED, CONTINUE TO beat FOR A FEW MORE MINUTES. ADD 1 tsp VANILLA. SPREAD MERINGUE LIGHTly OVER CAKE batter IN both PANS. BAKE FOR ABOUT 40 MINUTES.

AFTER THEY HAVE COOLED, PUT ONE LAYER UPSIDE DOWN ON SERVING PLATE. PUT WHIPPED CREAM ON LAYER THEN PUT CUT STRAWBERRIES (can be sweetened) ON THIS THEN PUT SECOND CAKE LAYER RIGHT SIDE UP ON TOP OF THIS WHIPPED CREAM AND STRAWBERRY FILLING. GARNISH TOP WITH DABS OF WHIPPED CREAM WITH WHOLE STRAWBERRIES ON TOP. REFRIGERATE OVERNIGHT SO THAT ALL THE LAYERS MELD TOGETHER. THIS SOUNDS MORE COMPLICATED THAN IT IS. ♡

blueberry BUCKLE
(from Teddy's kitchen)

KITCHEN MUSE, TEDDY GROBE, ALWAYS MADE THIS IN A VERY BATTERED MUCH LOVED TIN PAN. PERHAPS THIS WAS THE "X" FACTOR THAT MADE HER BUCKLE SO AMAZINGLY GOOD. IT ALSO COULD HAVE BEEN THE LOVE SHE POURED IN OR THE SPRINKLE OF UNUSUAL NUTS SHE ALWAYS ADDED OR THE FACT SHE THREW IN A DASH OF VARIOUS STRANGE COLORED LIQUEURS INTO EVERYTHING SHE BAKED.

3/4 cup SUGAR
1/4 cup BUTTER
ONE EGG
1/2 cup MILK
2 cups FLOUR
2 tsp bAKING POWDER
1/2 tsp SALT
1/2 cup SOUR CREAM
2 cups blueberries

MIX BUTTER AND SUGAR, THEN ADD THE EGG. ALTERNATE ADDING MILK AND FLOUR SIFTED WITH BAKING POWDER AND SALT. ADD THE SOUR CREAM AT THE END THEN FOLD IN THE blueberries. PUT IN GREASED PAN — A 9X13" PAN WILL WORK WELL.

SPRINKLE WITH CRUMB MIXTURE OF 1/2 CUP SUGAR : 1/3 CUP FLOUR : 1/2 tsp CINNAMON : 1/4 CUP SOFT BUTTER.

BAKE AT 375° FOR 25-35 MINUTES.

Blueberry CRUMB Cake

OUR THIRTY HIGHBUSH BLUEBERRY BUSHES WERE OUR FIRST GARDEN PROJECT HERE AT THE FARM, AND WE PLANTED THEM BEFORE WE EVEN BROKE GROUND FOR OUR FARM HOUSE. THEY NOW BEAR COPIOUS AMOUNTS OF BERRIES FOR FREEZING, COOKING, JAMS AND JUST PLAIN EATING STRAIGHT OFF THE BUSH.

THIS IS ONE OF OUR FAVORITE BLUEBERRY RECIPE. THE TANGY YOGURT CREAM IS JUST THE RIGHT BALANCE TO THE CAKE.

2 1/2 CUPS BLUEBERRIES
1/2 tsp. LEMON ZEST
2 1/4 CUP FLOUR
ONE CUP SUGAR
1 1/2 STICK UNSALTED BUTTER CUT IN PIECES
1 tsp. BAKING SODA
ONE EGG
HALF CUP PLAIN YOGURT
ONE tsp. FRESH LEMON JUICE.
TANGY YOGURT CREAM (RECIPE FOLLOWS)

PREHEAT OVEN TO 350 DEGREES. BUTTER 10" SPRINGFORM OR SIMILAR PAN. TOSS BLUEBERRIES WITH LEMON ZEST AND SET ASIDE. IN A LARGE BOWL COMBINE TWO CUPS FLOUR WITH SUGAR. RUB IN BUTTER UNTIL MIXTURE RESEMBLES COARSE MEAL. SET ASIDE 1 1/2 CUPS OF THE MIXTURE FOR CRUMB TOPPING. IN SMALL BOWL, ADD REMAINING FLOUR TO BAKING SODA AND THEN MIX INTO BOWL WITH MEALY MIXTURE. BLEND WELL.

BEAT EGG AND STIR IN YOGURT AND LEMON JUICE. ADD TO MEALY MIXTURE AND STIR BRIEFLY. FOLD IN ONE CUP OF THE BLUEBERRIES. SPREAD IN PREPARED PAN AND SCATTER REMAINING 1 1/2 CUP BLUEBERRIES ON TOP. SPRINKLE WITH CRUMB TOPPING AND BAKE FOR ABOUT 45-55 MINUTES. I FIND THIS THE TRICKIEST PART OF THIS CAKE. YOU DON'T WANT TO OVERCOOK IT BUT SOMETIMES THE OUTSIDE GETS DONE WELL BEFORE THE INSIDE. ERR ON THE SIDE OF UNDER COOKING AS IT IS MUCH BETTER MOIST. SERVE WITH THE FOLLOWING TANGY YOGURT CREAM: ONE CUP HEAVY CREAM: TWO TBS. SUGAR: ONE tsp. LEMON JUICE: 1/3 CUP YOGURT:

BEAT ALL INGREDIENTS UNTIL STIFF. COVER AND REFRIGERATE AT LEAST 30 MINUTES BEFORE SERVING.

Blueberry Cheesecake SQUARES

This is a beautiful and delicious dessert that cuts neatly into squares for a potluck or picnic. I have given directions for making a small batch of homemade jam to use, but store bought jam works just as well.

SHORT BREAD CRUST.
- 1¾ cups FLOUR
- ½ cup CONFECTIONER'S SUGAR.
- PINCH SALT.
- ONE CUP (TWO STICKS) BUTTER, AT ROOM TEMPERATURE.

CHEESECAKE FILLING
- ONE lb. (2 PACKAGES) CREAM CHEESE
- ½ CUP SUGAR
- 2 tsp VANILLA
- 2 EGGS

ONE CUP BLUEBERRY JAM OR TWO CUPS BLUEBERRY COOKED WITH ½ CUP SUGAR.

PREHEAT OVEN TO 300 DEGREES. BUTTER 9x13" PAN. MIX FLOUR SUGAR, SALT AND BUTTER TOGETHER AND PRESS INTO THE BOTTOM OF THE PAN. BAKE FOR 25-30 MINUTES UNTIL JUST BEGINNING TO BE SLIGHTLY GOLDEN BROWN. REMOVE AND COOL FOR HALF AN HOUR.

MIX CREAM CHEESE, SUGAR AND VANILLA UNTIL WELL BLENDED. ADD EGGS AND MIX UNTIL JUST COMBINED. POUR OVER COOLED CRUST.

IF YOU WANT TO USE FRESH BLUEBERRIES TO MAKE A QUICK JAM, MASH TWO CUPS OF BERRIES AND COOK ON MEDIUM HEAT FOR ABOUT FIVE MINUTES UNTIL BERRY MASH IS UNIFORMLY DEEP PURPLE. ADD HALF CUP SUGAR AND BRING TO BOIL AND BOIL ABOUT FIVE MINUTES. THIS MAKES ABOUT A CUP OF JAM. PUT DOLLOPS OF JAM WHILE STILL WARM ONTO THE CREAM CHEESE MIXTURE AND THEN SWIRL IN WITH A KNIFE. STORE BOUGHT JAM CAN BE HEATED UP SLIGHTLY SO IT SWIRLS INTO THE CHEESECAKE LAYER BETTER.

COOK FOR 35 MINUTES AT 300 DEGREES. REFRIGERATE UNTIL SERVING.

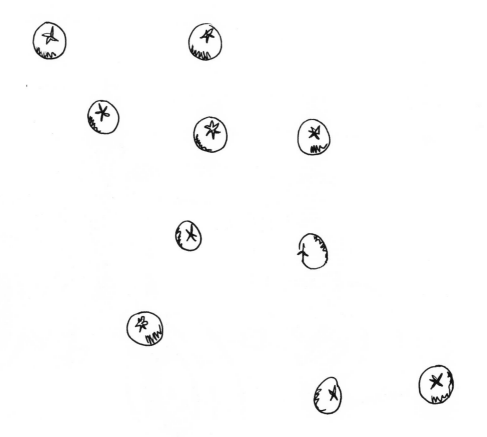

FRUIT COBBLER

THIS RECIPE WORKS WITH JUST ABOUT ANY MIXTURE OF FRUIT AND HAS A LOVELY UNUSUAL FLAVOR.

- 4 CUPS FRUIT BLACKBERRIES, BLUEBERRIES, SLICED PEACHES, OR PEARS OR ANY COMBINATION OF FRUIT.
- 2 CUPS SUGAR
- 1 CUP FLOUR
- 1 tsp BAKIN' POWDER
- ½ tsp CINNAMON
- ¼ tsp NUTMEG
- ¼ tsp SALT

- 1 CUP MILK
- ½ tsp VANILLA
- 1 STICK BUTTER, MELTED AND COOLED

IN BOWL TOSS TOGETHER FRUIT AND
HALF THE SUGAR. LET STAND FOR
30 MINUTES. IN BOWL SIFT TOGETHER
THE REMAINING SUGAR, FLOUR
BAKING POWDER AND SPICES. ADD
THE MILK AND VANILLA. STIR THE
MIXTURE UNTIL JUST COMBINED. POUR
MELTED BUTTER INTO 10" SQUARE
PAN. IF, LIKE ME, YOU DON'T HAVE A
10" SQUARE BAKING PAN JUST USE
A 9 X 13" AND KNOW THIS MAY GET
COOKED A LITTLE BIT FASTER. ADD
BATTER AND STIR TO COMBINE WITH
BUTTER. SPOON FRUIT OVER IT. BAKE
COBBLER IN A 350 DEGREE OVEN FOR
30 MINUTES, INCREASE HEAT TO 400
DEGREES AND BAKE COBBLER 10-15
MINUTES MORE OR UNTIL GOLDEN
ON THE EDGES. LET COBBLER COOL
FOR 20 MINUTES BEFORE SERVING.

fruit COMPOTE

WITH CASHEW CREAM

THIS RECIPE CAME FROM LONG TIME GREEN HOPE FARM FRIEND AND MIDWIFE PAM BECKER. SHE DELIVERED WILLIAM!

CASHEW CREAM

1/2 CUP CASHEWS
1/2 CUP ALMONDS
TWO Tbs. Maple Syrup
ONE tsp. VANILLA
WATER

PUT NUTS IN FOOD PROCESSOR, PROCESS UNTIL QUIET. ADD VANILLA AND SYRUP THEN ENOUGH WATER TO MAKE IT CREAMY. START WITH 2-3 Tbs OF WATER. YOU CAN MAKE THIS WITH ALL ALMONDS but ALL CASHEWS IS too GOOEY. SERVE CREAM OVER FRUIT.

3/4 lb MIXED DRIED PREFERABLY ORGANIC DRIED FRUITS SUCH AS PRUNES APRICOTS, CHERRIES AND PEARS.
ONE STICK CINNAMON
1/2 LEMON, ORGANIC WITH SEEDS REMOVED.
PUT ALL FRUIT IN A POT. ADD PLENTY OF WATER, 2-3 INCHES OVER THE TOP OF THE FRUIT. ADD CINNAMON AND LEMON BRING TO BOIL AND SIMMER 1/2 HOUR. LET SIT ANOTHER HOUR.

FRUIT PIZZA

SOMETIMES I double OR TRIPLE THIS RECIPE THEN ASK WHOMEVER IS HANGING AROUND TO EACH DECORATE A PIZZA. IT IS SURPRISING HOW DIFFERENTLY PEOPLE WILL DECORATE THEIR PIZZAS, but THEY ARE ALWAYS BEAUTIFUL!

CRUST:

3/4 cup butter
2/3 CUP SUGAR
2 CUPS FLOUR
1/4 CUP MILK.

BEAT butter AND SUGAR TOGETHER UNTIL LIGHT AND FLUFFY. COMBINE WITH FLOUR AND MILK AND MIX WELL. PRESS DOUGH ONTO A PIZZA PAN OR COOKIE SHEET. I USE PARCHMENT PAPER SO THE DOUGH DOESN'T STICK TO THE PAN AFTER IT IS COOKED. USING A COOKIE SHEET MEANS YOU CAN MAKE THE PIZZA IN SOME OTHER SHAPE THAN A CIRCLE. BAKE AT 400 DEGREES FOR 13-18 MINUTES UNTIL GOLDEN BROWN. COOL COMPLETELY BEFORE TOPPING WITH CREAM CHEESE FILLING AND FRUIT.

FILLING:

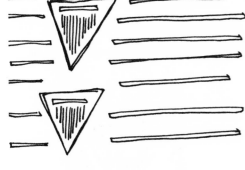

8 oz CREAM CHEESE
1/4 CUP SUGAR
1 tsp. GRATED LEMON RIND.
2 Tbs. SOUR CREAM
1/2 tsp VANILLA
FRUIT OF YOUR CHOICE
(WE OFTEN USE: blueberries, RASPBERRIES, RED AND GREEN GRAPES, KIWIS AND SLICED STRAWBERRIES.)

BEAT ALL INGREDIENTS UNTIL SMOOTH. POUR ON COOLED CRUST AND SPREAD ALMOST TO THE EDGES. ARRANGE ASSORTED FRUITS OF YOUR CHOICE OVER THE FILLING THEN DRIZZLE WITH THE FOLLOWING GLAZE. 1/2 CUP SUGAR 3/4 CUP ORANGE JUICE, 1 Tbs CORNSTARCH.

PUT SUGAR AND CORNSTARCH IN SMALL SAUCEPAN THEN ADD JUICE. BRING TO BOIL AND boil FOR TWO MINUTES. COOL FOR 10 MINUTES BEFORE USE.

LEMON
Squares

MAKE SHORTBREAD SQUARES FIRST. THESE CAN BE EATEN PLAIN OR MADE INTO LEMON SQUARES.

TWO CUPS SIFTED All PURPOSE FLOUR.
1/2 CUP SUGAR
ONE CUP (TWO STICKS) BUTTER AT ROOM TEMPERATURE.

PREHEAT OVEN TO 350 DEGREES COMBINE FLOUR AND SUGAR IN LARGE bowl. CUT butter INTO bowl AND MIX WITH YOUR FINGERS UNTIL MIXTURE FORMS A FINELY CRUMBLED DOUGH. SPREAD DOUGH ON UNGREASED 15 X 10" Jelly roll PAN PRESSING OR PATTING IT OUT UNTIL IT EVENly COVERS. IF USING FOR LEMON SQUARES bAKE UNTIL Lightly browNED 15-20 MINUTES. IF USING FOR Short-bread CONTINUE bAKING UNTIL THE CENTER IS COOKED THROUGH AND THE bottomed IS GOlDEN, ABOUT FIVE MINUTES LONGER. REMOVE AND SET ASIDE! LET COOL.

because these HAVE MORE LEMON IN THEM than the typical LEMON SQUARES, THESE ARE PARTICULARly WONDERFUL. MANY YEARS AGO, DEb CARDEN brought these SQUARES TO OUR ATTENTION by bRINGING AN ENORMOUS WARM TRAY OF THEM TO HER FIRST DAY OF WORK HERE AT THE FARM.

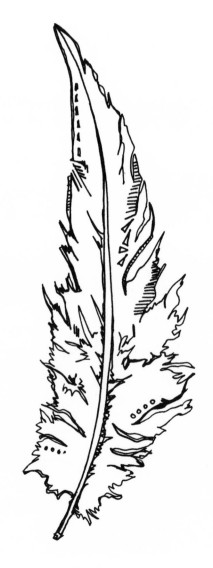

Lemon TOPPING

ONE BATCH BAKED AND COOLED
SHORTBREAD SQUARES
FOUR LARGE EGGS
TWO CUPS SUGAR
1/4 CUP ALL PURPOSE FLOUR
1 tsp. BAKING POWDER
1 Tbs. FINELY CHOPPED LEMON ZEST
1/2 CUP FRESH LEMON JUICE
10x SUGAR

PREHEAT OVEN TO 350 DEGREES.
CRACK EGGS INTO A LARGE bowl
AND BEAT WELL. ADD SUGAR, FLOUR,
BAKING POWDER, LEMON ZEST AND
JUICE. WHISK TO MIX. POUR OVER
SHORT BREAD, SPREADING EVENLY
AND BAKE UNTIL GOLDEN ON TOP
20-25 MINUTES. REMOVE AND
COOL IN PAN. WHEN COOL, SIFT
10x SUGAR OVER THE TOP, CUT
INTO SQUARES AND SERVE.

LEMON CAKE
WITH
Lemon ICING

LEMONS ARE VERY POPULAR HERE,
AND SOMETIMES WE EVEN HAVE LEMONS
TO USE FROM OUR GREENHOUSE LEMON
TREES!!

- half lb. UNSALTED BUTTER, SOFTENED
- TWO CUPS SUGAR
- THREE EGGS
- THREE CUPS FLOUR
- half tsp BAKING SODA
- half tsp. SALT
- ONE CUP BUTTERMILK
- ONE HEAPING Tbs. GRATED LEMON ZEST
- TWO Tbs. FRESH LEMON JUICE.

PREHEAT OVEN TO THREE HUNDRED AND TWENTY-FIVE DEGREES GREASE ANGEL FOOD TUBE PAN. CREAM BUTTER AND SUGAR UNTIL LIGHT AND FLUFFY. BEAT IN EGGS ONE AT A TIME. SIFT TOGETHER FLOUR, BAKING SODA, AND SALT. STIR IN DRY INGREDIENTS INTO EGG MIXTURE ALTERNATING WITH THE BUTTERMILK, beginning AND ENDING WITH DRY INGREDIENTS. ADD LEMON ZEST AND LEMON JUICE. BAKE ON MIDDLE RACK OF OVEN FOR ONE HOUR AND FIVE MINUTES OR UNTIL CAKE PULLS AWAY FROM THE SIDES OF THE PAN. COOL CAKE IN PAN FOR ten MINUTES THEN REMOVE FROM PAN AND DRIZZLE WITH GLAZE WHILE CAKE IS STILL WARM.

LEMON ICING

- ONE LB. CONFECTIONER'S SUGAR
- EIGHT Tbs. UNSALTED BUTTER
- THREE Tbs. (HEAPING Tbs.) GRATED LEMON PEEL.
- HALF CUP LEMON JUICE

CREAM BUTTER AND SUGAR THOROUGHLY then ADD LEMON ZEST AND JUICE. SPREAD ON WARM CAKE.

No bake blueberry PIE

HERE IS A blueberry RECIPE THAT REQUIRES NO baking AND USES A LOT OF FRESH berries. IT IS beautiful, AND EVERYONE LOVES IT. I HAVE will TO THANK HERE FOR SUGGESTING THE CREAM CHEESE Filling ON THE bottom OF THIS PIE. THIS LAYER MAKES ALL THE DIFFERENCE.

WILL LIKES THIS SERVED WITH Whipped CREAM WHICH DOES ADD FURTHER GLORY TO AN ALREADY GLORIOUS PIE.

ONE baked bottom PIE CRUST FOR DEEP DISH 9" PIE PLATE
FIVE CUPS blueberries SOME TO be COOKED, SOME USED FRESH
1½ CUP SUGAR plus ¼ CUP SUGAR
1½ CUP WATER
FIVE Tbs CORNSTARCH
EIGHT OZ. CREAM CHEESE, ROOM TEMPERATURE.
ONE tsp. GRATED LEMON RIND
ONE tsp. VANILLA

BAKE A bottom CRUST FOR A PIE. I COOK AN UNBAKED PIE CRUST AT 450° FOR 10-15 MINUTES. I USE PIE WEIGHTS FOR THE FIRST FIVE OR SO MINUTES THEN REMOVE THESE AND WATCH THE PIE CRUST CAREFULLY UNTIL IT IS GOLDEN BROWN.

MIX ONE CUP WATER WITH 1½ CUP blueberries IN A MEDIUM SAUCEPAN. SQUASH THE berries. HEAT THIS UP TO A SIMMER THEN ADD ½ CUP WATER MIXED WITH 1½ CUP SUGAR AND THE CORNSTARCH. BRING THIS TO A BOIL, STIRRING CONSTANTLY AND boil FOR ABOUT A MINUTE UNTIL MIXTURE HAS THICKENED. SET ASIDE TO COOL.

MIX CREAM CHEESE WITH REMAINING ¼ CUP SUGAR, LEMON RIND AND VANILLA. SPREAD ON THE BOTTOM OF COOLED PIE CRUST. SPRINKLE THIS CREAM CHEESE MIXTURE WITH 3 CUPS FRESH blueberries. POUR OVER THIS THE COOLED COOKED berries MIXTURE. SPRINKLE WITH THE LAST ½ CUP OF blueberries. CHILL.

—191—

MERINGUE WITH BLUEBERRIES, Lemon Curd AND WHIPPED CREAM

THIS IS A SENSATIONAL COMBINATION AND VERY BEAUTIFUL.

MERINGUE: SIX EGG WHITES, ROOM TEMPERATURE ARE BEST.
TWO CUPS SUGAR
1 tsp. BAKING POWDER
VERY LARGE PINCH OF CREAM OF TARTAR.
2 tsp. VINEGAR
2 tsp. VANILLA

BEAT EGG WHITES UNTIL STIFF THEN ADD SUGAR SIFTED WITH CREAM OF TARTAR AND BAKING POWDER, ONE TABLESPOON AT A TIME. ADD VINEGAR AND VANILLA. BEAT FOR 15 MINUTES FROM START TO FINISH. I USE A FOOD PROCESSOR WITH A WHISK ATTACHMENT FOR THIS! PUT A PIECE OF PARCHMENT PAPER ON A COOKIE SHEET AND FORM A CIRCLE WITH THE MERINGUE ON THE PAPER. BUILD UP THE EDGES A BIT SO THERE WILL BE A HOLLOW IN THE CENTER OF THE MERINGUE. YOU CAN ALSO FILL A PIZZA PAN OR LARGER CIRCULAR CAKE PAN IF YOU WANT A MORE PERFECT CIRCLE, but USE THE PARCHMENT PAPER IN ANY CASE. BAKE AT 275 degrees FOR 1 HOUR. COOL THEN REFRIGERATE FOR AT LEAST 4 hours BEFORE ASSEMbling.

Lemon Curd:

10 EGG YOLKS
1½ CUPS SUGAR
¾ CUP FRESH LEMON JUICE, STRAINED.
¾ CUP (1½ STICK) COLD BUTTER.

IN A MEDIUM SAUCEPAN, WHISK TOGETHER THE YOLKS, SUGAR AND LEMON JUICE UNTIL SMOOTH. PUT ON LOW HEAT AND COOK, WHISKING CONSTANTLY, UNTIL THE MIXTURE STARTS TO THICKEN. DO NOT BOIL! THIS SHOULD TAKE ABOUT 10 MINUTES. REMOVE FROM HEAT AND let COOL FOR 10 MORE MINUTES. WHISK IN THE BUTTER A little bit AT A TIME, UNTIL All butter IS MELTED AND THE CURD IS SMOOTH. Place CURD IN A GLASS DISH WITH PLASTIC wrap ON THE top SO A SKIN DOES NOT FORM then PUT IN THE REFRIGERATOR. IF YOU DO NOT USE ALL THE LEMON CURD WITH MERINGUE, THE LEFTOVER CURD WILL last a MONTH IN THE REFRIGERATOR.

ASSEMBLY: SPREAD MERINGUE WITH LEMON CURD THEN GENEROUSLY SPRINKLE WITH blueberries. WHIP TWO CUPS OF WHIPPING CREAM. ADD A FEW TEA SPOONFULS OF CONFECTIONER'S SUGAR AND SOME VANILLA TO THE WHIPPED CREAM AT THE END OF THE WHIPPING PROCESS then put ON THE berry LAYER. FINISH by SPRINKLING A FEW MORE berries ON THE WHIPPED CREAM. WHEN YOU CUT INTO THIS, IT IS SUCH A PRETTY SIGHT.

>>> RHUBARB crisp WITH VANILLA SAUCE (CUSTARD)

Filling >>> : TWO lbs RHUBARB. SLICE INTO 3/4" PIECES. ONE CUP SUGAR 2 Tbs. FLOUR GRATED RIND OF ONE LEMON. 1/2 tsp. NUTMEG

PREHEAT OVEN TO 375 DEGREES.

RHUBARB IS A BEAUTIFUL PLANT OF GREAT WORTH IN ANY GARDEN. WE HAVE TWO BIG PLANTS IN OUR ROSE GARDEN AND ANOTHER LONE WOLF DOWN IN THE BERRY PATCH. WE HARVEST PLENTY OF RUBY RED STALKS IN EARLY SUMMER THEN ENJOY RHUBARB'S BEAUTIFUL FLOWERING STALKS ATOP ITS GORGEOUS LEAVES LATER IN THE SEASON.

MIX RHUBARB, SUGAR, FLOUR, LEMON RIND AND NUTMEG. SET ASIDE FOR 15 MINUTES.

TOPPING >>> ONE CUP FLOUR 2/3 DARK BROWN SUGAR. HALF CUP UNSALTED BUTTER.

IN BOWL MIX TOGETHER FLOUR AND SUGAR. ADD BUTTER AND WORK IN. PUT RHUBARB MIXTURE IN BAKING DISH THEN TOP WITH TOPPING. DO NOT PRESS DOWN TOPPING. BAKE 40 MINUTES.

VANILLA CUSTARD SAUCE

2 cups milk
5 egg yolks
1/3 cup sugar
2 tsp. vanilla

SCALD THE MILK IN HEAVY SAUCE-PAN. WHISK TOGETHER YOLKS AND SUGAR IN A BOWL THEN ADD HALF THE SCALDED MILK, STIRRING WELL. WHISK IN REST OF MILK AND PUT EVERYTHING BACK IN SAUCEPAN. COOK OVER MEDIUM LOW HEAT, STIRRING CONSTANTLY UNTIL SAUCE COATS THE BACK OF A SPOON. IT IS WORTH BEING PATIENT HERE TO GET A SMOOTH, ELEGANT SAUCE.

IF THE SAUCE BOILS, IT WILL CURDLE. BUT NO WORRIES — YOU CAN SAVE THE SAUCE by PUTTING IT IN A BLENDER AND BLENDING ON HIGH SPEED. CURDLED OR NOT, ADD VANILLA TO YOUR SAUCE AFTER YOU HAVE TAKEN IT OFF HEAT. SERVE SAUCE WITH WARM OR COLD CRISP.

PUMPKIN Cake

OVER THE YEARS WE HAVE GROWN A LOT OF PUMPKINS. THE GREAT THING ABOUT THIS RECIPE IS THAT YOU CAN ADD EXTRA COOKED PUMPKIN TO THE CAKE, AND WHILE THIS MAKES THE CAKE MORE LIKE A SOLID PUDDING THAN A CAKE, THE CAKE IS STILL DELICIOUS AND YOU HAVE USED UP MORE PUMPKIN INVENTORY!!

4 EGGS
1 1/4 CUP SUGAR
1/2 CUP OIL
2 1/2 CUPS COOKED PUMPKIN (OR MORE)
2 CUPS FLOUR
2 tsp BAKING POWDER
2 tsp CINNAMON
1/2 tsp BAKING SODA

BAKE A WHOLE PIE PUMPKIN OR SQUASH IN THE OVEN AT 350° FOR 1-2 HOURS UNTIL IT IS REALLY SOFT AT WHICH POINT IT WILL BE EASY TO PEEL AND THE PUMPKIN FLESH WILL BE READY TO USE IN THIS CAKE.

BEAT EGGS, SUGAR, OIL AND PUMPKIN TOGETHER THEN ADD DRY INGREDIENTS.

MIX WELL AND BAKE IN 9×13 INCH PAN AT AT 350° FOR 25-30 MINUTES OR LONGER IF YOU HAVE ADDED A LOT OF EXTRA PUMPKIN. FROST WITH BUTTER CREAM OR CREAM CHEESE FROSTING.

short CAKE
FOR

STRAW- BERRY
short CAKE

This is A better shortcake recipe than Any OTHERS I have tried. It should be good, given its ingredients!

🍓 TWO CUPS FLOUR
🍓 1/4 CUP SUGAR
🍓 FOUR tsp. baking POWDER
🍓 ONE stick butter
🍓 3/4 CUP CREAM (HALF AND HALF WORKS FINE)

cut in butter to flour, SUGAR AND BAKING POWDER UNTIL CONSISTENCY IS like that OF OATMEAL. ADD 3/4 CUP CREAM. MIX UNTIL JUST blended. ROll out OR JUST PlOP OUT APPROXIMATELY 6-8 biscuits onto Parchment LINED COOKIE sheet. COOK at 450° FOR ABOUT ten MINUTES UNTIL JUST FAINTLY GOLDEN BROWN.

SOUR CHERRY PIE

SOUR CHERRIES ARE A MARVELOUS FRUIT. THEY ARE A LUMINOUS RED, A JOY TO PICK, NOT SO VERY HARD TO PIT AND SIMPLY SPLENDID TO COOK WITH. WE FILL OUR FREEZER WITH PITTED CHERRIES AS WELL AS FROZEN BLUE-BERRIES.

CHERRY TREES GROW VERY FAST SO IT IS NEVER TOO LATE TO PLANT A LOVELY MONT-MORENCY CHERRY. YOU'LL HAVE MORE CHERRIES than YOU Can IMAGINE before you KNOW It, AND THE BIRDS WILL LOVE YOU FOR PLANT-ING this TREE AS THEY WILL EAT EVERY LAST CHERRY YOU DON'T PICK AND SOME YOU might have PICKED IF THEY hadn't GOTTEN THERE FIRST!!

PASTRY FOR TWO PIE CRUSTS

filling:
- 1 1/4 CUPS SUGAR
- 1/2 CUP FLOUR
- 1/2 tsp. SALT
- 5 CUPS PITTED SOUR CHERRIES
- 1/2 tsp ALMOND EXTRACT
- 2 Tbs. butter
- TUBE OF ALMOND PASTE (OPTIONAL but WORTH USING)
- 1 EGG YOLK
- 1 Tbs. WATER

PRE HEAT OVEN TO 400 DEGREES. PUT bottom CRUST INTO 9" DEEP PIE PLATE AND SLICE OR GRATE ALMOND PASTE EVENIy ONTO THE bottom CRUST. IN A LARGE bowl, MIX TOGETHER SUGAR, FLOUR AND SALT THEN ADD CHERRIES AND ALMOND EXTRACT. TURN CHERRY MiXTURE INTO PIE PLATE, MOUNDING Filling IN THE MIDDLE. DOT WiTH butter THEN TOP WITH CRUST, SEAL AND CRIMP. CUT VENTS IN CENTER OF Pie then lightly brush With GLAZE MADE FROM EGG YOIk MIXED WiTH Water.

BAKE 40-45 MINUTES UNTIL GOLDEN brown. I bAKE THiS ON A COOKIE SHEET. IN CASE THE filling OOZES OUT While THE PIE IS COOKiNG. THIS IS GREAT WiTH VANilla ICE CREAM OR JUST PLAIN, EVEN FOR bREAKFAST.

SOUR CHERRY COBBLER FROM
∴ TEDDY ∴

Cherries

ONE CUP SUGAR
ONE TBS. CORNSTARCH
ONE CUP BOILING WATER
THREE CUPS PITTED SOUR
    CHERRIES
½ tsp CINNAMON
ONE TBS. BUTTER

TOPPING

ONE CUP FLOUR
ONE TBS. SUGAR
ONE AND ½ TSP BAKING
    POWDER
ONE tsp. SALT
SIX TBS. BUTTER
½ CUP MILK

IN A SAUCEPAN, MIX SUGAR AND CORNSTARCH THEN STIR IN BOILING WATER. BRING TO BOIL AND BOIL FOR ONE MINUTE THEN ADD SOUR CHERRIES AND CINNAMON PUT IN A SMALL PYREX DISH ABOUT 10 X 6 X 2 OR A CERAMIC DISH THAT CAN GO IN THE OVEN. DOT WITH BUTTER.

FOR TOPPING MIX DRY INGREDIENTS THEN CUT IN BUTTER. ADD THE MILK AND THEN PLOP THE BATTER ON TOP OF THE CHERRIES. BAKE FOR 30 MINUTES AT 400 DEGREES.

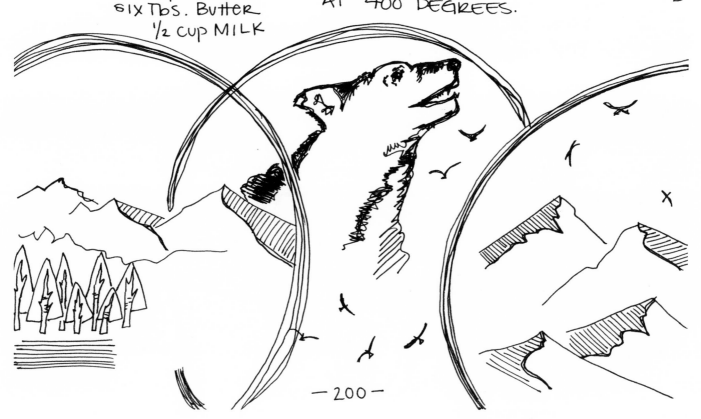

strawberry Rhubarb Pie

I never quite feel comfortable with combinations of fruits that are not in season together. I want to put a disclaimer on this sort of dish saying something like, "Yes, yes, I know that not until about twenty years ago could these strawberries and pears be bedfellows."

Luckily, strawberries and rhubarb are actually available in the garden at the same time, and they taste like they were meant to be together.

PIE PASTRY FOR TWO CRUSTS

One and a half cup sugar
(a little more if you prefer a sweeter pie)
Two third cup flour
Four cups sliced strawberries
Four cups sliced rhubarb
One tsp. grated orange peel.
Two Tbs. butter.
Preheat oven to four hundred degrees.

Put uncooked pie crust in nine inch pie plate.

Mix rhubarb, strawberries, flour, sugar and orange peel together and pour into pie shell. Dot with butter and cover with top crust. Crimp edges and cut vents in top crust then bake for forty-five minutes.
Cook on a cookie sheet to avoid spills.

TRIFLE

I DON'T QUITE KNOW HOW to EXPLAIN OUR FAMILY'S FIXATION WITH ENGLISH CLASSICS, but WE LOVE THEM. THIS TRIFLE MAKES AN APPEARANCE AT ALMOST ALL HOLIDAYS AND MANY birthdays AS WELL.

CAKE: HOT MILK CAKE FROM THIS COOKBOOK OR SPONGE CAKE OF YOUR CHOICE.

RASPBERRY JAM.

❂ PASTRY CREAM ❂

1½ CUP MILK

½ CUP SUGAR

¼ CUP FLOUR

3-4 WELL BEATEN EGG YOLKS OR TWO EGGS AND TWO EGG YOLKS

ONE tsp. VANILLA.

A DAY BEFORE YOU WANT TO EAT THE TRIFLE, MAKE A SPONGE CAKE. THE HOT MILK CAKE RECIPE WORKS WELL BAKED IN A 9×13" PAN. WHEN CAKE IS COOL, CUT IT INTO SLICES SORT OF LIKE SMALL SLICES OF BREAD AND MAKE THESE PIECES INTO SANDWICHES by SPREADING RASPBERRY JAM BETWEEN TWO SLICES. SET ASIDE.

SCALD MILK. MIX SUGAR, FLOUR AND EGGS IN THE TOP OF A DOUBLE BOILER. BEAT THIS MIXTURE UNTIL LIGHT THEN SLOWLY ADD SCALDED MILK. STIR UNTIL ALL IS WELL BLENDED AND COOK, STIRRING CONSTANTLY IN DOUBLE BOILER OVER BUT NOT IN BOILING WATER UNTIL CUSTARD BEGINS TO THICKEN. REMOVE FROM HEAT AND CONTINUE TO STIR TO RELEASE STEAM SO SKIN WON'T FORM ON CUSTARD. ADD A GENEROUS TEASPOON OF VANILLA AND COOL MIXTURE WITH PLASTIC WRAP ON TOP, AGAIN TO PREVENT SKIN FROM FORMING.

ASSEMBLY:

CAKE SANDWICHES
PASTRY CREAM
3/4 CUP SHERRY
FRUITS SUCH AS PEACHES, BLUEBERRIES, STRAWBERRIES, RASPBERRIES, COOKED PEARS.
TWO CUPS WHIPPING CREAM
TOASTED SLIVERED ALMONDS.

IN A GLASS BOWL IF YOU HAVE ONE OR DEEP BOWL, PUT HALF OF THE RASPBERRY JAM CAKE SANDWICHES. SPRINKLE HALF OF THE SHERRY ON CAKE SLICES. TOP WITH HALF THE FRUIT. TOP WITH HALF THE CUSTARD. PLACE SECOND HALF OF CAKE SLICES ON TOP OF CUSTARD. SPRINKLE WITH THE REST OF THE SHERRY THEN ADD THE REST OF THE FRUIT THEN THE CUSTARD. COVER AND REFRIGERATE OVERNIGHT.

BEFORE SERVING, WHIP TWO CUPS WHIPPING CREAM AND SPREAD ON TOP OF TRIFLE. GARNISH WITH TOASTED SLIVERED ALMONDS.

COOKIES AND bARS

butterscotch
BROWNIES

THESE ARE RIDICULOUSLY EASY TO MAKE AND DISAPPEAR VERY FAST.

1 CUP UNSALTED BUTTER

2 CUPS WELL PACKED LIGHT BRONN SUGAR

2 EGGS, BEATEN

1½ CUP FLOUR

2 tsp BAKING POWDER

1 tsp. SALT

1 tsp VANIIIA

3/4 CUP COARSELY CHOPPED WALNUTS

HEAT OVEN^to 350 DEGREES AND BUTTER A 8x10 PAN. MELT BUTTER IN MEDIUM SAUCEPAN ON LOW HEAT. REMOVE FROM HEAT AND ADD SUGAR. COMBINE WELL AND COOL TO ROOM TEMPERATURE. ADD EGGS, MIXING WELL. SIFT FLOUR, BAKING POWDER AND SALT THEN ADD TO SAUCEPAN, STIRRING AS YOU ADD. MIX WELL AND THEN STIR IN VANIIIA AND WALNUTS.

BAKE 35-45 MINUTES OR UNTIL A KNIFE COMES OUT CLEAN. WE TEND TO LIKE THEM UNDERCOOKED.

chocolate CHIP COOKIES a la DEB CARDEW

THESE ARE slightly DIFFERENT THAN TOLL HOUSE AND WHAT A DIFFERENCE IT MAKES!

½ lb UNSALTED butter AT ROOM TEMPERATURE

1 cup LIGHT brown SUGAR.

¾ GRANULATED SUGAR.

2 LARGE EGGS AT ROOM TEMPERATURE

1 GENEROUS tsp. VANILLA EXTRACT

2 CUPS UNBLEACHED ALL PURPOSE FLOUR

¾ tsp. bAKING SODA

2 cups SEMI SWEET CHOCOLATE CHIPS

1-2 CUPS CHOPPED WALNUT, PECANS OR CASHEWS

PREHEAT OVEN to 350 DEGREES

CREAM butter AND SUGARS UNTIL LIGHT.

ADD EGGS AND VANILLA BEING CAREFUL TO NOT OVER-BEAT.
SIFT IN DRY INGREDIENTS AND MIX WELL. STIR IN CHIPS AND NUTS.

DROP LARGE Tbs. OF DOUGH ONTO COOKIE SHEET. BAKE 12 MINUTES OR UNTIL COOKIES ARE BROWN AT EDGE BUT SOFT IN THE MIDDLE.

COOL COOKIE SHEET BETWEEN BATCHES.

Enjoy

Before Green Hope Farm, I ran a bakery with a friend. It was called Best Friends Bakery and had a brief but glorious reign. Eventually we hung up our aprons and returned to our gardens but not before we learned a thing or two about cookies.

CHOCOLATE CHOCOLATE CHIP COOKIES

These cookies were particularly popular. They make great ice cream sandwich cookies if the dough is made into large cookies.

One cup butter
1 1/2 cup sugar
two eggs
two tsp vanilla
two cups flour
2/3 cup Hershey's baking cocoa powder
3/4 tsp baking soda
two cups chocolate chips.

Cream butter and sugar. Add eggs and vanilla, beating until light and fluffy. Combine flour, cocoa and baking soda. Add to creamed mixture. Stir in chips. To make small cookies drop one inch balls on ungreased cookie sheet. Bake at 350 degrees for 8-10 minutes. Larger cookies for ice cream sandwiches will take more time to cook.

Choco Mint
COOKIES

First made famous by
our Aunt Susan Sheehan
and then by Ben who is
now expected to make
these at Christmas
for a few thousand
serious cookie fans.

- Three fourths cup butter
- One and a half cup dark brown sugar.
- Two Tbs. water
- Twelve oz semi sweet chocolate bits
- Two eggs
- Two and a half cups flour
- One and one fourths tsp. baking soda
- half tsp. salt
- One pound andes mints

In large saucepan at low heat cook
butter, sugar and water until butter is
melted. Add chocolate bits until partially
melted and remove from stove. Continue
to stir until chocolate bits are melted. Pour
in bowl and let stand ten minutes til
slightly cooled. At high speed use mixer
to add eggs one at a time. Reduce speed
to low and add dry ingredients until
just blended. Chill one hour. Make
walnut size balls and place two-three
inches apart on cookie sheet. Bake at
three fifty for twelve-thirteen minutes.
Put an andes mint on each cookie. After
three-four minutes spread melted mint
on cookie.

COCONUT
MACADAMIA NUT
BARS

WHAT'S NOT TO LOVE ABOUT COCONUT, BUTTER, SUGAR AND MACADAMIA NUTS COOKED TOGETHER?

FOR THE SHORTBREAD LAYER:
TWO CUPS FLOUR
TWO STICKS BUTTER
2/3 CUPS CONFECTIONER'S SUGAR
1/2 tSp. SALT

PRE HEAT OVEN TO 350°

PUT SHORTBREAD LAYER IN 9×13" PAN AND BAKE FOR 20 MINUTES UNTIL GOLDEN BROWN.

FOR THE TOPPING:
1/2 STICK UNSALTED BUTTER
1/2 CUP FIRMLY PACKED BROWN SUGAR
ONE CAN COCO LOPEZ (CREAM OF COCONUT)
2 TbS LEMON JUICE
2 2/3 CUPS FLAKED COCONUT
1 1/3 CUPS MACADAMIA NUTS

MAKE SHORTBREAD TOPPING. WHILE SHORTBREAD IS COOKING. MELT BUTTER OVER LOW HEAT THEN REMOVE PAN FROM HEAT. WHISK IN BROWN SUGAR UNTIL DISSOLVED AND THEN WHISK IN COCO LOPEZ AND LEMON JUICE. STIR IN FLAKED COCONUT AND NUTS. POUR TOPPING OVER SHORTBREAD. REDUCE TEMPERATURE TO 325 AND BAKE UNTIL GOLDEN BROWN 45-50 MINUTES.

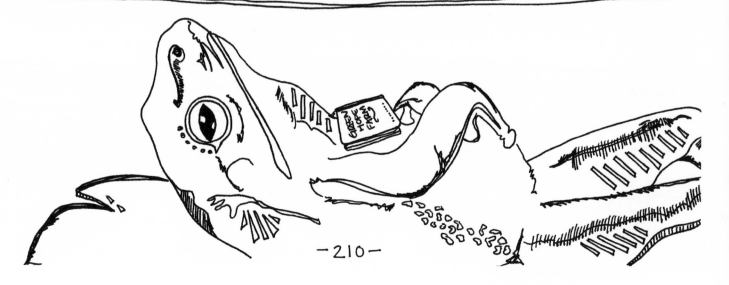

DATE BARS

• 1½ CUP PITTED DATES • 1½ CUPS ORANGE JUICE •
2½ CUPS FLOUR • ½ tsp SALT • 1½ CUPS FIRMLY
PACKED LIGHT BROWN SUGAR • 3 STICKS BUTTER,
CUT INTO PIECES • 1 CUP SWEETENED FLAKED
COCONUT • 1 CUP CHOPPED WALNUTS •
1½ CUPS OLD-FASHIONED ROLLED OATS •

IN A SAUCEPAN, SIMMER THE DATES IN
ORANGE JUICE STIRRING FOR 30 MINUTES
OR UNTIL MIXTURE HAS THICKENED. IN
A BOWL COMBINE THE FLOUR, SALT,
SUGAR, AND BLEND IN THE BUTTER
UNTIL MIXTURE IS CRUMBLY. STIR
IN THE COCONUT, THE WALNUTS AND
THE OATS. PRESS HALF THE MIXTURE
IN A 9×13 INCH PAN. PAT FLAT WITH
A SHEET OF PARCHMENT PAPER. SPREAD
DATE MIXTURE OVER THE DOUGH MIXTURE
TO WITHIN AN HALF INCH OF THE EDGES.
TOP WITH REMAINING DOUGH MIXTURE
AND FLATTEN LIGHTLY. BAKE IN A PRE-
HEATED OVEN, 350 DEGREES, FOR 45
MINUTES OR UNTIL GOLDEN. COOL
BEFORE CUTTING BARS.

doppelganger bars

A FRUIT BAR WE SNACKED ON AT A NEARBY FARM STAND LED TO MANY UNSUCCESSFUL ATTEMPTS TO RECREATE THE EXACT RECIPE WE HAD TASTED. IT ALSO RESULTED IN ELIZABETH CREATING THIS bar. WE named them Doppelganger BARS AS THEY ARE like the ORIGINAL FARM STAND BARS but NOT THE SAME.

ONE batch OF SUGAR COOKIES—
RECIPE ON PAGE —222—
1½ CUP STRAWBERRY OR OTHER FRUIT JAM.

PREHEAT OVEN TO 350°.

BUTTER OR LINE A JELLY ROLL PAN (10" X 15") WITH PARCHMENT PAPER. PRESS HALF SUGAR COOKIE DOUGH INTO the bottom OF THE PAN. SPREAD WITH the JAM. CRUMBLE THE REST OF THE DOUGH ON TOP OF THE JAM COVERING MOST OF THE JAM. bAKE FOR 35-40 MINUTES UNTIL GOLDEN BROWN.

Fruit Butter Bars

Because we have so many apple and pear trees, we make apple and pear butter as well as canned applesauce and canned pears. This recipe will work with any fruit butter you have on hand. When I gave this recipe to a friend, she made these with pumpkin butter and brought me a sample. They were delicious!

• • • • • •

One package yellow cake mix
Half cup melted butter
Three eggs
One to one and a half cups fruit butter
Half cup milk
One Tbs. flour
One cup sugar
1/4 cup soft butter
One tsp. cinnamon

• • • • • • • • •

Measure one cup cake mix and set aside. Stir remaining cups cake mix with melted butter and one of the eggs. Press in the bottom of the 9 x 13" pan. Mix fruit butter with milk and last two eggs. Pour over base layer in pan. Mix reserved cake mix with flour, sugar, butter and cinnamon and crumble on top of fruit filling. Bake at 350 degrees for 35-40 minutes.

• • • • • • • • •

MARY ANN'S
REFRIGERATOR
COOKIES

THIS COOKIE RECIPE COMES FROM JIM'S MOM MARY ANN. JIM'S SISTER SUSAN ALWAYS INCLUDES BOTH THE VANILLA AND CHOCOLATE VARIETY IN HER GIFT BASKETS OF CHRISTMAS COOKIES. THESE SEEM LIKE PLAIN, ORDINARY, UNASSUMING COOKIES BUT THEY ARE ALWAYS THE FIRST TO GO. THERE IS SOMETHING ABOUT THEM THAT IS IRRESISTIBLE.

- VANILLA VARIETY • 4 CUPS FLOUR • 1 tsp BAKING POWDER • 1/4 tsp BAKING SODA • 1 tsp. SALT • 1 1/3 CUP BUTTER • 1 CUP BROWN SUGAR • 2/3 CUP WHITE SUGAR • 2 EGGS • 1 1/2 tsp. VANILLA •

CREAM BUTTER AND SUGAR ADD EGGS & VANILLA. SIFT TOGETHER DRY INGREDIENTS THEN MIX WITH BUTTER MIXTURE. SHAPE DOUGH INTO ROLLS ABOUT ONE INCH IN DIAMETER WRAP IN PARCHMENT PAPER AND REFRIGERATE. SLICE 1/4 INCH THICK SLICES AND BAKE AT 400 DEGREES FOR 5-8 MINUTES.

FOR CHOCOLATE VARIETY, USE ALL WHITE SUGAR AND ADD 4 OUNCES MELTED AND COOLED BAKING CHOCOLATE TO THE DOUGH AT THE END.

MINT BROWNIES

These brownies are very popular at all social events, meetings and bake sales in our small town. I think there might be a riot if there was a gathering and no one brought a batch of these brownies.

- Two squares unsweetened chocolate
- Half cup butter
- Two eggs, beaten
- One cup sugar
- One fourth tsp. peppermint flavoring
- Half cup flour
- Dash salt

Melt chocolate and butter in double boiler. Cool, add eggs, sugar, flavoring, flour and salt. Cook in nine inch square pan for twenty to twenty-five minutes at three hundred and fifty degrees. Cool.

MINT FROSTING

- Two Tbs. butter
- One cup confectioner's sugar
- One Tbs. cream
- Half tsp. peppermint flavoring
- Few drops green food coloring

Spread on cooled brownies. Refrigerate

You might want to double this frosting recipe! I do!

glaze

- One square unsweetened chocolate.
- One Tbs. butter.

Melt in a double boiler then spread over mint frosting then refrigerate brownies.

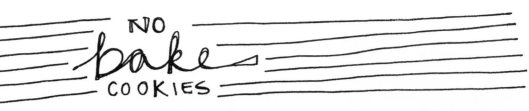

NO bake COOKIES

A LANKY SIX FOOT TWO, WILLIAM
PREFERS A COOKIE that COMES
TOGETHER FAST AND PROVIDES A
high VOLUME OF CALORIES.
THIS MAKES THESE HIS FAVORITE
COOKIE, ESPECIALLY IF HE IS COOKING,
AS THEY CAN BE READY IN A MATTER
OF MINUTES.

- FOUR OZ. BUTTER. (8 TBS.)
- half CUP MILK.
- TWO CUPS SUGAR.
- ONE CUP SEMISWEET
  CHOCOLATE CHIPS.
- THREE - FOUR TBS.
  PEANUT BUTTER.
- THREE CUPS ROLLED OATMEAL,
  OLD FASHIONED OR QUICK.
- ONE tsp. VANILLA.

Place chocolate chips, PEANUT butter, OATS AND VANILLA IN A LARGE
bowl. COMBINE BUTTER, MILK, SUGAR IN SAUCEPAN and bring to a
rolling boil. BOIL FOR ONE MINUTE. Combine WITH OATMEAL mix well.
DROP SPOONFULLS ON PARCHMENT PAPER. THESE WILL SET UP INTO FIRM COOKIES.

the OFFICIAL OFFICE

COOKIE

(LAURA'S FAMOUS! OATMEAL RAISIN COOKIES)

We have WORKED OUR WAY through ABOUT thirty thousand of STAFFER LAURA CARPENTER'S BUTTERY OATMEAL COOKIES. This IS REALLY NOT too MUCH OF AN EXAGGERATION!! DUE to the PLEAS OF hungry OFFICE MATES, LAURA AS WELL AS LIZZY BAKE THESE UP FOR US MOST EVERY WEEK!!

- ONE CUP UNSALTED BUTTER
- ONE CUP SUGAR
- ONE CUP BROWN SUGAR
- 2 LARGE EGGS
- TWO-THREE tsp VANIlla
- ONE tsp. BAKING SODA
- ONE tsp BAKING POWDER
- ONE tsp. KOSHER SALT
- TWO CUPS FLOUR
- THREE CUPS OATS (NOT INSTANT)
- 1½ CUPS RAISINS

CREAM together butter AND SUGARS then ADD EGGS AND VANIlla, MIX-ING WELL. SIFT baking SODA, baking POWDER, SALT AND FLOUR then ADD TO the butter AND SUGAR MIX. STIR IN OATS AND RAISINS. A TWO tbs SCOOP OF DOUGH MAKES A NICE SIZE COOKIE. BAKE AT 350° FOR 11-13 MINUTES.

SHORtBREAD WITH CHOCOLATE CHIP TOPPING

WHEN LIZZY WAS PREG-
NANT WITH GRACE, SOME
OF THE STAFF STOPPED
bRINGING IN THEIR OWN
lunches because THEY
KNEW LIZZY WOULD BE
BAKING UP A STORM
EACH DAY AND THEY
WOULD BE THE bENE-
FICIARIES. THESE
SHORTBREAD SQUARES
WERE FREQUENTLY ON
THE DOCKET.

ONE CUP BUTTER
ONE CUP SUGAR
ONE tsp. VANillA
ONE EGG YOLK
TWO CUPS FLOUR

CREAM butter AND SUGAR.
BLEND IN EGG YOLK AND
VANillA THEN ADD FLOUR.
BAKE FOR 15-20 MINUTES
AT 350 DEGREES UNTIL
JUST GOLDEN BROWN.
IMMEDIATELY PUT TWO
CUPS OF CHOCOLATE
CHIPS ON SHORT-
BREAD. SPREAD THEM
EVENLY OVER SHORTBREAD
WHEN MELTED.

SOUR Cream CASHEW COOKIES

My sister in law, Susan Sheehan, bakes cookies each holiday season for an armada of friends and family. We all have our favorite from Susan's vast repertoire. These are mine!!

Two cups sifted flour: one tsp. baking powder: 3/4 tsp. baking soda: one egg: half cup soft butter: one cup packed brown sugar: one tsp. vanilla: half cup sour cream: 1½ cups salted cashews, chopped:

Sift flour, baking powder and baking soda together then set aside. Beat eggs, butter, sugar, vanilla and sour cream together well. Chop nuts coarsely and add to above. Add flour mixture to batter and drop by tsp full on cookie sheet. Bake ten minutes. Makes about 7 dozen. Cool and frost with: three Tbs. light cream: 1 tsp. vanilla: 4 oz. cream cheese: two Tbs. butter: three cups confectioner's sugar: green food coloring: put all but sugar in blender, food processor or kitchen aid mixer. Blend on slow until smooth. Add one cup of sugar at a time. Run on high speed until smooth. Add a few drops of green food coloring to make pale green frosting.

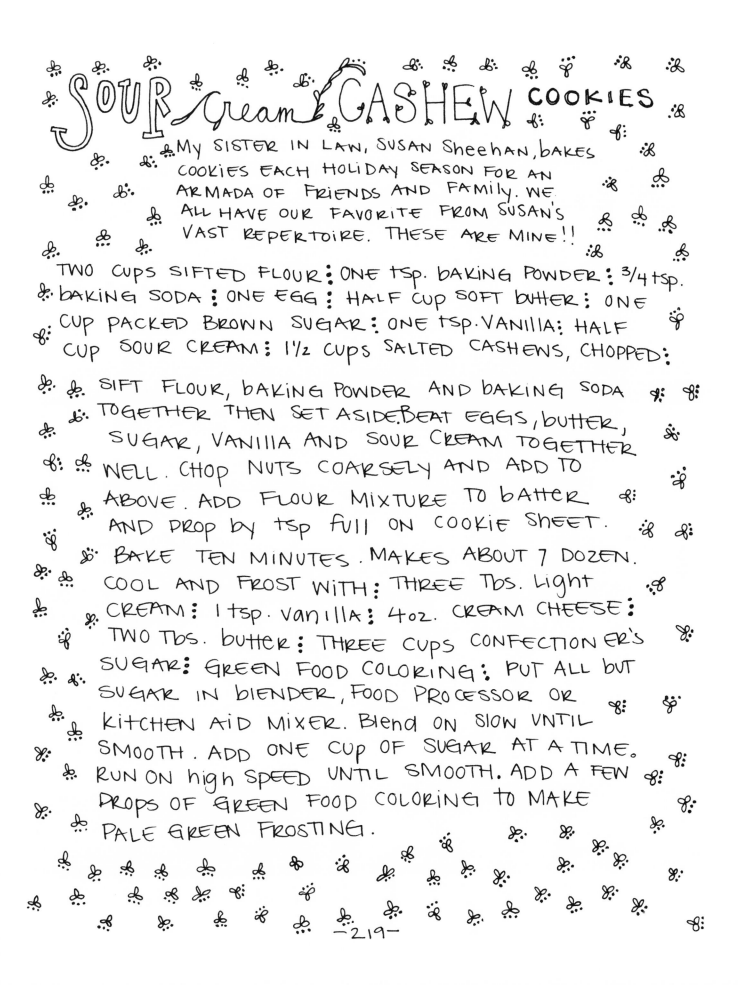

TOFFEE

Bark.

When William is making dessert, he either makes these or his TRADEMARK NO BAKES.

- Saltine Crackers
- one cup butter (2 sticks)
- ONE CUP BROWN SUGAR.
- 12 oz. bag semi sweet
- CHOCOLATE Chips.

LINE A JELLY ROll PAN (10"x15") WITH PARCHMENT PAPER. then COVER the bottom OF the PAN IN A SINGLE layer OF SALTINE CRACKERS.

I have a well-loved jelly roll pan because my Mother in law taught me how to make WONDERFUL Jelly rolls when I was first Married. the LIP on a jelly ROll PAN IS the most important thing here as it keeps the sweet sauce on the CRACKERS, NOT ON YOUR OVEN FLOOR.

In honor of SWEET MAY MAY

bring to boil butter and
BROWN SUGAR AND BOIL
FOR THREE MINUTES.
Stir Often

— — — — — —

POUR this CARAMEL OVER SALTINES
AND BAKE FOR ten MINUTES IN A 350°
OVEN.

TOP WITH LARGE bAG OF
CHOCOLATE Chips AND SPREAD
Evenly —— WHEN MELTED.

REFRIGERATE FOR at
LEAST AN
HOUR.

Sugar Cookies

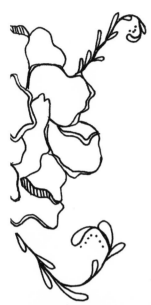

I WAS GIVEN MY BELOVED GRANDMOTHER'S COPY OF "THE JOY OF COOKING". ON THE PAGES OF HER COOKBOOK, SHE WROTE COMMENTS ABOUT RECIPES, SO WHENEVER I USE THE COOKBOOK, I FEEL LIKE I AM GETTING A VISIT WITH HER. IN FRONT OF THIS RECIPE SHE HAS WRITTEN A big "NO". THEY REALLY ARE THAT IRRESISTIBLE. HER "NO" HAS NOT STOPPED US, AND I DOUBT IT STOPPED HER!

1 1/2 cup butter
2 1/2 cups SUGAR
TWO EGGS
TWO EGG YOLKS
SIX CUPS ALL PURPOSE FLOUR SIFTED WITH 1/2 tsp SALT.
TWO TSP VANILLA

CREAM butter UNTIL SOFT THEN ADD SUGAR. BEAT IN EGGS AND YOLKS ONE AT A TIME. ADD VANILLA. STIR SIFTED FLOUR MIXTURE SLOWLY INTO butter MIXTURE SOME OF THE FLOUR MAY be KNEADED IN by HAND. CHILL FOR SEVERAL HOURS, ROll OUT ON PARCHMENT PAPER. ROll DOUGH THINLY AND USE COOKIE CUTTERS TO CUT OUT COOKIES. BAKE IN A 400° OVEN FOR ABOUT 8 MINUTES. DEPENDING ON PERSONAL PREFERENCES. HALF OF US LIKE THEM SOFT AND THE OTHERS LOVE THEM A LittLE CRISP. THESE CAN bE FROSTED WITH A BUTTERCREAM FROSTING.

OTHER desserts

— MUD — PIE —

WE NOW MAKE THIS RECIPE IN CUPCAKE TINS WITH CUPCAKE PAPERS AS IT IS MUCH EASIER TO SERVE THIS WAY. BEN REALLY DOES ASK FOR THIS EACH BIRTHDAY AND NOW DOES NOT HAVE TO SAW US OFF A PIECE OF PIE FROM A TOO FROZEN ICE CREAM PIE.

CRUST

- half PACKAGE THIN CHOCOLATE WAFERS, GROUND FINE.
- ONE FOURTH CUP UNSALTED BUTTER, MELTED

MIXED WAFERS WITH MELTED BUTTER. PRESS INTO NINE INCH PAN OR INTO INDIVIDUAL CUPCAKE PAPERS IN A CUPCAKE TIN. CHILL IN FREEZER FOR HALF AN HOUR.

FILLING AND TOPPING

- HIGH QUALITY COFFEE ICE CREAM (BEN PREFERS STARBUCKS)
- FUDGE SAUCE - THE CHARLESTON CHOCOLATE SAUCE IN THIS BOOK WORKS WELL. — PAGE 229
- ONE CUP HEAVY CREAM, WHIPPED.

LET ICE CREAM STAND AT ROOM TEMPERATURE FOR TEN MINUTES OR UNTIL SOFT ENOUGH TO SPREAD WITH- OUT BEING MELTED. PIE PLATE WILL TAKE ABOUT HALF GALLON OF ICE CREAM. SPREAD ICE CREAM OVER CRUST. SMOOTH AND FREEZE FOR ONE HOUR UNTIL ICE CREAM IS FROZEN SOLID. SPREAD ROOM TEMPERATURE FUDGE SAUCE ON ICE CREAM. TOP WHIPPED CREAM AND SERVE.

BÊTE
noire

ONE CUP WATER
3/4 CUP SUGAR
NINE Tbs. butter
18 oz. bAKING CHOCOLATE,
    CHOPPED
Six LARGE EGGS
    Whipped.

THIS FLOURLESS DARK CHOCOLATE CAKE RECIPE COMES FROM THE ZEALAND APPALACHIAN MOUNTAIN HUT IN THE WHITE MOUNTAINS OF NEW HAMPSHIRE. Alli, STAFFER AND illustRATOR OF THIS book, HAS A PACK OF FRiENDS WORKING IN VARIOUS huts IN THE white MOUNTAINS. SHE CLiMbs up the MOUNTAINS TO SEE THEM ON MANY A WEEKEND. HER FRiEND AT ZEALAND SHARED the RECiPE, NOTING. "IT's A FAVORiTE AMONG US AND OUR GUESTS AT THE HUT."

PREHEAT OVEN TO 350 DEGREES.
    BUTTER A 10" SPRING FORM PAN.

COMBINE WATER AND SUGAR IN SAUCEPAN AND bRING TO BOIL OVER MEDIUM HEAT. STIRRING UNTIL CLEAR. SET ASIDE.

MELT buTTER IN LARGE SAUCEPAN OVER LOW HEAT. ADD CHOCOLATE AND WhiSK UNTIL SMOOTH. WhiSK IN SUGAR SYRUP AND COOL SLightly.

ADD Whipped Eggs AND WhiSK UNTIL blENDED. POUR INTO PREPARED PAN. PLACE PAN IN LARGE ROASTING PAN. ADD ENOUGH WATER TO SUbMERGE 1/2 WAY up SPRING FORM PAN. BAKE UNTIL CAKE NO LONGER SHAKES WHEN JiGGLED, ABOUT 50 MINUTES.

COOL COMPlETEly IN PAN (ABOUT TWO HOURS). UNSPRING PAN. TOP WITH WhiPPED CREAM, bERRiES OR ROASTED COCONUT.

bermuda Ginger
MOUSSE.

Lynn Tidman wrote our flower essence labels for twenty years. That was well over a million labels!! We called her "our lady of labels". I don't know what her tired hands called us! Lynn grew up in Bermuda and took me on many wonderful trips to her childhood home. That was the origins of our Bermuda flower essences. She had so many friends on the island with so many beautiful gardens and the semi-tropical flowers offered amazing strengths so different from our temperate flowers. We had such fun meeting the flowers and making them into flower essences. This old Bermuda recipe reminds me of Lynn and her island home.

-226-

ONE QUART HEAVY CREAM
HALF CUP GRANULATED SUGAR
TWO Tbs. CHOPPED CRYSTALLIZED GINGER
ONE CUP COCONUT FLAKES
TWO CUPS WALNUTS, CHOPPED
TWO Tbs. SCOTCH.
NINE Tbs. DRAMBUIE (SCOTCH
LIQUEUR)
ONE BOX OF GINGER SNAPS.

WHIP CREAM UNTIL VERY STIFF THEN ADD
SUGAR. FOLD IN GINGER, COCONUT, WALNUTS
SCOTCH AND DRAMBUIE. MIX WELL.

IN A PRETTY BOWL (A CLEAR GLASS
BOWL OR TRIFLE BOWL WORKS WELL)
LAYER GINGERSNAPS AND CREAM
MIXTURE, REPEATING LAYERS UNTIL
ALL THE CREAM MIXTURE IS USED.
END WITH A LAYER OF CREAM. COVER
WITH PLASTIC WRAP AND REFRIGERATE
AT LEAST EIGHT HOURS, BETTER YET.
OVERNIGHT.

ButterScotch
SAUCE.

this easy and delicious butterscotch SAUCE is my SISTER IN LAW KATY Sheehan's family RECIPE from her GRANDMOTHER Bishop.

KATY WAS OUR first baby-sitter When Ben was a toddler then When She GREW UP she MaRRied JIM'S BROTHER Stephen. They LIVE ACROSS TOWN FROM US With their TWO giRIS in a house IN the WOODS WITH a *lovely* — POND.

AND A HALF
- ONE^ CUP bROWN SUGAR
- half CUP CORN SYRUP
- four tbs butter
- PINCH OF SALT
- half cup EVAPORATED MiLK.
- HALF tsp Vanilla

In heavy bottomED Saucepan, mix SUGARS ADD butter AND COOK UNtIL Soft ball Stage, 234° ADD milk and cool.

add VANILLA.

...CHARLESTON...
...CHOCOLATE SAUCE...

THIS WAS THE CHOCOLATE SAUCE THAT MY FAMILY MADE WHEN I WAS A CHILD. IT IS RUNNY but hAS A WONDERFUL FLAVOR. THE RECIPE CAME FROM THE JUNIOR LEAGUE'S "CHARLESTON RECEIPTS COOK BOOK".

TWO OUNCE bAKING CHOCOLATE

ONE CUP BOILING WATER

ONE tsp. VANIIIA

FOUR Tbs. butter

ONE CUP SUGAR

PINCH OF SALT

MELT CHOCO-LATE IN A DOUBLE BOILER. ADD BUTTER AND STIR. WHEN MELTED ADD THE BOILING WATER, STIRRING CONSTANTLY. ADD THE SUGAR. TAKE OFF DOUBLE bOILER AND PUT DIRECTIY OVER THE HEAT, BRING to A BOIL AND COOK FOR FIVE MINUTES. ADD SALT AND VANILLA.

CHOCOLATE
cake
FOR THE AGES.

THE ONLY CHOCOLATE CAKE RECIPE YOU WILL EVER NEED!! IT HAS BEEN THE CAKE OF CHOICE AT COUNTLESS BIRTHDAY PARTIES AT THE FARM AS WELL AS THREE WEDDINGS! ONE BRIDE SPENT THE DAY AFTER HER WEDDING SITTING ON HER FRONT PORCH EATING LEFTOVER CAKE TO HER HEART'S CONTENT.

TWO CUPS FLOUR
TWO CUPS SUGAR
3/4 CUP COCOA POWDER
ONE tsp. BAKING POWDER
TWO tsp. BAKING SODA
TWO EGGS
ONE CUP MILK
ONE CUP OIL
TWO tsp. VANILLA
ONE CUP COFFEE.

MIX ALL INGREDIENTS WELL. THE BATTER WILL SEEM RUNNY... BAKE IN BUTTERED ANGEL FOOD TIN OR BUNDT PAN. AT 350 DEGREES FOR 40-50 MINUTES. DO NOT OVERCOOK.

MEGA-MOCHA FROSTING
A REGULAR VANILLA FROSTING IS WONDERFUL WITH THIS CAKE BUT SO IS THIS MOCHA FROSTING.

ONE lb. CONFECTIONER'S SUGAR
ONE Tbs. COCOA
3/4 CUP BUTTER
TWO Tbs. INSTANT COFFEE GRANULES DISSOLVED IN THREE Tbs. CREAM OR MILK

BEAT WITH ELECTRIC BEATERS. ADD MORE CREAM AS NECESSARY.

FLAN

I SPENT A PART OF MY CHILDHOOD IN MEXICO CITY. EVEN BEFORE MIGUEL JOINED OUR FAMILY, FLAN WAS A MAINSTAY.

1½ CUP SUGAR, DIVIDED
SIX EGGS
GENEROUS PINCH OF SALT
FOUR CUPS WHOLE MILK, SCALDED
ONE tsp. VANILLA.

PREHEAT OVEN TO 300 DEGREES. HEAT ¾ CUP OF SUGAR IN A SMALL HEAVY PAN, STIRRING CONSTANTLY WITH A WOODEN SPOON UNTIL THE SUGAR MELTS AND IS FREE FROM LUMPS AND TURNS A LIGHT CARAMEL IN COLOR. POUR CARAMEL EVENLY OVER THE BOTTOM OF AN OVEN PROOF CERAMIC TWO QUART DISH THAT YOU KNOW CAN HANDLE THE HOT CARAMEL.

BEAT EGGS SLIGHTLY WITH REMAINING SUGAR AND SALT. ADD THE SCALDED MILK SLOWLY WHILE STIRRING, THEN ADD VANILLA. STRAIN THIS AS YOU POUR IT INTO THE PAN WITH THE CARAMEL. SET THIS DISH INTO A SECOND PAN OF HOT WATER. THE WATER SHOULD BE ALMOST LEVEL WITH THE TOP OF THE DISH. BAKE UNTIL A KNIFE COMES OUT CLEAN WHEN INSERTED IN THE CENTER OF THE FLAN ABOUT 45 MINUTES TO AN HOUR.

TO SERVE, RUN A KNIFE AROUND EDGE OF CUSTARD, PUT PLATTER ON TOP OF DISH AND INVERT. FLAN SHOULD COME OUT REVEALING A BEATIFUL FIRM CUSTARD WITH A LOVELY LIQUID CARAMEL DRIZZLING DOWN THE SIDES.

EMILY QUIMBY'S

Steamed Christmas
PUDDING

WHEN I MOVED to THE TINY VILLAGE OF MERIDEN, NH IN 1979 THERE WAS A WONDERFUL GROUP OF ZESTY OLDER WOMEN HERE TO INSPIRE ME. TEDDY WAS ONE OF THEM. EMILY WAS ANOTHER. SHE MAPLE SUGARED WITH PANACHE, MAKING UP TO 100 GALLONS OF SYRUP A SEASON WITH HER BEAUTIFUL TIN EVAPORATOR. SHE HAD SHEEP - LOTS OF THEM, EACH WITH A SWISS BELL AROUND ITS NECK THAT MADE A DIFFERENT MUSICAL NOTE. SHE HAD BEEN JAILED FOR HER POLITICAL BELIEFS - MORE THAN ONCE. SHE WAS BUSY HELPING MANY CAMBODIAN BOAT PEOPLE SETTLE IN THIS AREA. SHE ALSO HAD A BIG CHRISTMAS PARTY EACH YEAR WHERE SHE SERVED A MASSIVE NUMBER OF THESE AMAZING STEAMED PUDDINGS. PEOPLE ARRIVING AT THE PARTY WOULD RACE TO THE PUDDINGS, LOOKING FOR THEIR ANNUAL FIX OF THIS TREAT.

ONE CUP SUGAR

1½ CUP CHOPPED SUET

ONE CUP SOFT BREAD CRUMBS

HALF CUP LIGHT MOLASSES (I SUBSTITUTE MAPLE SYRUP HERE)

HALF CUP SHREDDED CITRON

TWO CUPS FLOUR SIFTED WITH ONE tsp. EACH OF CLOVES, BAKING SODA, CINNAMON AND SALT.

TWO LARGE APPLES, PEELED AND CUT FINE

THREE LARGE BEATEN EGGS.

COMBINE All INGREDIENTS, PUT IN A WELL GREASED STEAMED PUDDING MOLD OR LARGE COFFEE CAN SEALED WITH ALUMINUM FOIL. STEAM OVER but NOT IN boiling WATER FOR THREE HOURS. I USE A RACK IN THE bottom OF A LARGER POT TO SET the MOLD ON, SO IT IS ABOVE the WATER. BE SURE TO KEEP ENOUGH WATER IN THE bottom OF YOUR PAN FOR THE WHOLE THREE HOURS. IF YOU NEED to REHEAT THE PUDDING, PUT MOLD IN hot WATER. SERVE WARM WITH the FOLLOWING WARM SAUCE.

SAUCE: Melt Slowly ONE CUP White SugAR IN ONE CUP butter. WHEN SUGAR IS THOROUGHLY MELTED beAT IN 2-3 WELL beATEN EGGS WITH AN ELECTRIC MIXER. FLAVOR WITH VANIllA.

FRESH GINGER CAKE

DEB CARDEN WORKED HERE DURING THE WEEK THEN SOLD HER BAKED GOODS AT THE LOCAL FARMER'S MARKET ON THE WEEKENDS. SHE MUST HAVE MADE A COUPLE THOUSAND OF THESE CAKES OVER THE YEARS, EVERY ONE OF THEM DELICIOUS.

FOUR OUNCES FRESH GINGER ◀ ONE CUP MILD MOLASSES ▲ ONE CUP SUGAR ◀ ONE CUP VEGETABLE OIL PREFERABLY PEANUT ▲ TWO AND A HALF CUPS FLOUR ▲ ONE tsp. CINNAMON ▲ HALF tsp. GROUND CLOVES ▲ HALF tsp. GROUND BLACK PEPPER ▲ ONE CUP WATER ▲ TWO tsp. BAKING SODA ◀ TWO EGGS, ROOM TEMPERATURE ◀

PREHEAT OVEN TO 350°. LINE 9 OR 9 1/2 INCH SPRING-FORM PAN WITH PIECE OF PARCHMENT PAPER ON BOTTOM. PEEL AND GRATE OR FINELY CHOP GINGER. MIX TOGETHER MOLASSES, SUGAR, AND OIL. IN ANOTHER BOWL MIX FLOUR, CINNAMON, CLOVES AND PEPPER. BRING WATER TO A BOIL IN A SAUCEPAN THEN STIR IN BAKING SODA AND THEN MIX THE HOT WATER INTO THE MOLASSES MIXTURE. STIR IN THE GINGER. GRADUALLY WHISK IN THE DRY INGREDIENTS INTO THE BATTER. ADD THE EGGS AND CONTINUE MIXING UNTIL EVERYTHING IS THOROUGHLY COMBINED. BAKE ONE HOUR OR UNTIL CAKE SPRINGS BACK LIGHTLY WHEN PRESSED OR TOOTHPICK INSERTED IN CENTER COMES OUT CLEAN.

GRAPE NUT PUDDING

THIS VERY OLD FASHIONED
DESSERT RANKS HIGH AS
A COMFORT FOOD AMONG
ALL THE SHEEHANS.

...THREE EGGS....
....THREE FOURTHS CUP SUGAR....
....THREE CUPS MILK....
....ONE CUP GRAPE-NUTS....
CEREAL
....ONE FOURTH tsp. NUTMEG....
....ONE tsp VANILLA....

BEAT EGGS THEN ADD SUGAR
SLOWly. ADD MILK, GRAPE-NUTS
CEREAL, NUTMEG AND VANILLA.
LET STAND FIFTEEN MINUTES IN
BUTTERED BAKING DISH. BAKE
IN PAN OF HOT WATER AT THREE
HUNDRED AND FIFTY FOR FORTY-
FIVE MINUTES OR UNTIL A KNIFE
INSERTED COMES OUT CLEAN.

HONEY
MOUSSE
WE LOVE HONEY BEES!

FOR DECADES WE HAD beehives NESTLED UNDER THE WINDOWS OF OUR OFFICE WHERE WE COULD WATCH THE BEE TRAFFIC AND LISTEN TO THEIR LOVELY NOISE.

THEN A VERY BIG AND VERY DETERMINED BEAR BEGAN TO FREQUENT THE HIVES FOR NIGHTTIME SNACKS. WE TRIED VARIOUS THINGS TO GET HIM TO CEASE AND DESIST BUT NOT SURPRISINGLY, ME IN MY NIGHTGOWN THROWING APPLES DIDN'T WORK. NOR did ELaborate protective FENCING. FINALLY WE MOVED THE HIVES TO THE SECOND STORY OF OUR BARN. FROM THIS NEW PERCH, THE HONEY BEES CONTINUE TO GIVE US A SHINING EXAMPLE OF SELFLESS SERVICE AND COOPERATIVE COMMUNITY.

THE BELOVED HONEY BEES HELP US BALANCE THE ENERGIES OF THE LAND, POLLINATE OUR CROPS AND BRING JOY. THEIR HONEY IS A TREASURE. While MOST OF THE HONEY WE COLLECT GOES ON TOAST OR IN TEA, WE DO MAKE DESSERTS WITH HONEY. THIS HONEY MOUSSE IS A LOVELY CELEBRATORY dISH OF THE MOST beautiful COLOR AND SUBLIME TASTE.

3/4 CUP HONEY
SIX BEATEN EGG YOLKS.
TWO CUPS HEAVY CREAM.

IN THE TOP OF A DOUBLE BOILER, COMBINE HONEY AND YOLKS AND COOK OVER BOILING WATER, STIRRING CONSTANTLY, UNTIL THE CUSTARD COATS THE SPOON. PUT PAN IN A BOWL OF ICE CUBES AND STIR UNTIL COOL. CUSTARD WILL THICKEN SLIGHTLY. WHIP CREAM UNTIL IT HOLDS PEAKS AND FOLD IN HONEY MIX. PUT THE MOUSSE IN A SERVING BOWL AND FREEZE WITHOUT STIRRING FOR 3-4 HOURS. EVEN AFTER 24 HOURS IN THE FREEZER THIS WILL HAVE THE WONDERFUL CONSISTENCY OF SOFT ICE CREAM.

honeycomb PUDDING

THIS IS A TRIED AND TRUE MAPLE SYRUP RECIPE THAT HAS BEEN IN the family AT LEAST SEVENTY-FIVE YEARS♡.

- half cup to ONE CUP SUGAR (I TEND TO USE LESS SUGAR but THE honeycomb IS BETTER WITH *all* THE SUGAR) ♫
- ONE CUP FLOUR
- ONE CUP MAPLE SYRUP
- HALF CUP BUTTER
- HALF CUP LUKE WARM MILK
- ONE tsp BAKING SODA
- FOUR EGGS, WELL BEATEN.

MIX SUGAR AND FLOUR then ADD MAPLE SYRUP. MELT BUTTER IN MILK AND ADD BAKING SODA. COMBINE MIXTURES, BEAT thoroughly AND then ADD EGGS. TURN IN TO BUTTERED BAKING DISH AND BAKE at THREE HUNDRED AND FIFTY DEGREES FOR FORTY-FIVE MINUTES TO AN HOUR. DO NOT OVERCOOK. AND SERVE WITH *cream*.

This is a classic cake recipe from my mother in law, Mary Ann. It is versatile, easy to make and is great for birthdays or for use in a trifle.

HOT milk CAKE

- ◇ THREE EGGS ◇
- ◇ 1 ½ cup SUGAR ◇
- ◇ 1 ½ cup flour ◇
- ◇ 1 ½ tsp. baking POWDER ◇
- ▷ ¼ tsp SALT ◇
- ◇ 1 tsp Vanilla ◇
- ◇ ¾ cup Milk ◇
- ◇ 3 Tbs butter ◇

BEAT EGGS UNTIL VERY LIGHT AND FLUFFY. THEY SHOULD BE the CONSISTENCY OF A MERINGUE. BEAT IN THE SUGAR GRADUALLY. STIR IN DRY INGREDIENTS AND VANILLA. ADD butter to Milk AND BRING to A FOAMING BOIL. STIR IMMEDIATELY INTO the bAtter. BAKE AT 350 DEGREES FOR 20-25 MINUTES.

MAPLE SUGARING AND OUR MAPLE SYRUP RECIPES

WE MAKE MAPLE SYRUP EACH SPRING IN A TYPICAL NORTH COUNTRY BACKYARD SUGARING OPERATION.

WE PUT IN ABOUT FORTY TAPS ON MUCH LOVED MAPLE TREES IN THE NEIGHBORHOOD THEN HANG OLD-FASHIONED SAP BUCKETS ON THESE TREES. WE HAVE A BIG COLLECTING TANK THAT GETS PUT IN THE BACK OF OUR PICKUP TRUCK DURING SUGARING SEASON, AND WE COLLECT SAP IN THIS TANK EVERY AFTERNOON.

DURING THE DAY AND INTO THE EVENING WE BOIL THE COLLECTED SAP IN A SMALL WOOD FIRED EVAPORATOR RIGHT OUTSIDE THE OFFICE DOOR. WE FINISH THE SYRUP IN THE KITCHEN WHERE WE CAN GET THE DENSITY JUST RIGHT AND HAVE LOTS OF MESSY SPILLOVERS WHEN WE LOSE OUR FOCUS ON THE BOIL.

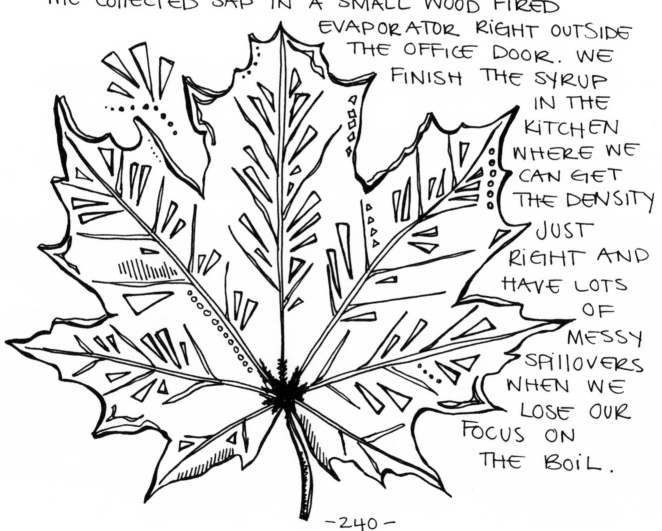

Maple sugaring is one of our happiest times of the year. It gets us outside during a time of the year when we have serious cabin fever, and it also provides us with ten to fifteen gallons of wonderful maple syrup depending on the season. No matter the vagaries of the particular season, when maple sugaring begins there is usually a lot of snow on the ground and by its end there are crocus and spring peepers in the gardens. It really takes us through mud season to glorious spring!

The following are some of our favorite maple syrup recipes.

HONEY COMB PUDDING

MAPLE MUFFINS WITH MAPLE GLAZE

MAPLE DREAM

APPLE MAPLE CUSTARD PIE

MAPLE
dream

BEN AND I MAKE THIS ABOUT ONCE A YEAR AND THEN EAT THE WHOLE thing by OURSELVES RATHER A DECADENT MOMENT BUT ONE WE ENJOY.

FIRST LAYER.

2 CUPS FLOUR
1 CUP CHOPPED NUTS
1 CUP BUTTER

COMBINE AND PRESS INTO A 9 X 13 INCH PAN. BAKE AT 350° FOR 20 MINUTES. COOL.

SECOND LAYER

1 CUP CONFECTIONERS SUGAR.
8 oz CREAM CHEESE
ONE CUP WHIPPED CREAM

BLEND AND SPREAD ON FIRST LAYER.

THIRD LAYER

3 CUPS MAPLE SYRUP
3 EGGS
2/3 CUP FLOUR

=FOR THIRD LAYER=
COMBINE AND BEAT EGGS AND FLOUR. MIX WITH WARM SYRUP. BRING to boil BEATING ALL THE TIME TO PREVENT STICKING. COOL AND SPREAD ON SECOND LAYER.

=FOR FOURTH LAYER=
TOP WITH WHIPPED CREAM.

INDIAN PUDDING

THIS IS A SLIGHTLY UNTRADITIONAL VERSION OF A VERY TRADITIONAL NEW ENGLAND DESSERT. IT IS UNUSUAL BECAUSE IT DOES NOT COOK AS LONG AS MOST INDIAN PUDDINGS COOK BUT TASTES AS GOOD.

- THREE CUPS MILK
- ONE FOURTH CUP CORNMEAL
- TWO EGGS, BEATEN
- HALF CUP DARK MOLASSES
- ONE FOURTH CUP SUGAR
- HALF tsp. SALT
- ONE tsp. CINNAMON
- THREE FOURTHS tsp GINGER.
- HALF CUP WHEAT GERM.

SCALD MILK. GRADUALLY ADD CORNMEAL AND COOK TEN MINUTES, STIRRING FREQUENTLY. REMOVE FROM HEAT. COMBINE EGGS, MOLASSES SALT, SUGAR AND SPICES. BEAT SLIGHTLY AND ADD THIS TO THE MILK MIXTURE. STIR IN WHEAT GERM. POUR IN LIGHTLY GREASED ONE AND HALF QUART DISH. PLACE IN PAN OF HOT WATER AND BAKE AT THREE HUNDRED AND TWENTY-FIVE DEGREES FOR AN HOUR AND FIFTEEN MINUTES OR UNTIL KNIFE COMES OUT CLEAN. SERVE WARM WITH CREAM, WHIPPED CREAM OR VANILLA ICE CREAM.

MOCHA cream ROLL

THIS MAKES A GREAT buche de NOEL, A
TRADITIONAL CHRISTMAS DESSERT IN FRANCE.

ONE CUP SIFTED CAKE FLOUR OR 7/8TH CUP
SIFTED ALL PURPOSE FLOUR :||| 1/4 CUP
UNSWEETENED COCOA POWDER :||| ONE
tsp. bAKING POWDER :||| THREE EGGS :|||
ONE CUP SUGAR :||| 1/3 CUP COLD
BREWED COFFEE :||| ONE tsp. VANiIIA

LiNE A JeIIy ROII PAN, (10" x 15") WITH PARCHMENT
PAPER THEN butter THE PAPER. SIFT FLOUR, COCOA
AND bAKING POWDER TOGETHER AND SET ASIDE.
BEAT EGGS WITH AN ELECTRIC MIXER UNTIL
THICK AND CREAMY. GRADUAIIy ADD SUGAR,
bEATiNG CONSTANTIy UNTIL MiXTURE IS VERy
THiCK. STiR IN COFFEE AND VANiIIA THEN ADD
FLOUR. SPREAD bATTER IN PAN. BAKE AT
375 DEGREES FOR 10-12 MINUTES. LOOSEN
CAKE. INVERT ONTO A DiSHCLOTH LIGHTIy
DUSTED WITH CONFECTiONER SUGAR. GENTIy
REMOVE PARCHMENT PAPER THEN ROII UP
CAKE IN DiSHCLOTH SPRiNKIiNG WITH
CONFECTiONER'S SUGAR. YOU ROII UP THE CAKE
WHIIe IT IS STILL WARM SO IT WILL COOL
AND SET IN THiS ROIIED SHAPE.

coffee cream filling

2 tsp. INSTANT COFFEE POWDER
1½ CUPS HEAVY CREAM
½ CUP CONFECTIONER'S SUGAR

DISSOLVE COFFEE IN CREAM by SETTING IN REFRIGERATOR FOR AN HOUR OR SO. THEN WHIP CREAM WITH SUGAR UNTIL STIFF. UNROLL COMPLETELY COOLED CAKE AND SPREAD FILLING ON CAKE AND REROLL. PUT SEAM ON THE BOTTOM.

Mocha frosting

2 CUPS CONFECTIONER'S SUGAR
4 Tbs. COCOA POWDER
4 Tbs MELTED BUTTER
2 tsp VANILLA
COFFEE.

MIX SUGAR, COCOA AND BUTTER AND VANILLA WITH ENOUGH COFFEE TO MAKE A FROSTING OF THE PROPER CONSISTENCY.

:III VARIATION OF CHOCOLATE GINGER ORANGE ROLL :III
SUBSTITUTE ONE tsp. GROUND GINGER FOR COFFEE IN CAKE AND USE WATER INSTEAD OF COFFEE.

filling ...SUBSTITUTE 3 tsp FROZEN ORANGE JUICE CONCENTRATE, ⅓ CUP CHOPPED CRYSTALLIZED GINGER AND 3 Tbs. GRATED ORANGE PEEL FOR COFFEE GRANULES.

frosting ... USE MILK INSTEAD OF COFFEE AS LIQUID.

MISSISSIPPI

MUD *cake*

IN THE EARLY EIGHTIES
BEFORE WE STARTED
GREEN HOPE FARM, JIM
AND I TAUGHT AT
KIMBALL UNION ACADEMY,
THE VERY SAME SCHOOL
WHERE OUR SON BEN
NOW TEACHES. THIS
DECADENT DESSERT
WAS SOMETHING WE
WOULD MAKE FOR THE
KIDS IN OUR DORM. THE
STUDENTS LIKED IT SO
MUCH THAT ONE OF THEM
CONVINCED HIS FATHER
TO BUY ONE AT A
SCHOOL FUNDRAISER FOR
$400. I MADE THE CAKE
AND PROMPTLY DROPPED
IT FACE DOWN ON THE
GROUND. THEN I HAD TO
START ALL OVER AGAIN!

YES, A PAN OF THIS WEIGHS
ABOUT THIRTY POUNDS, AND
IT'S ABOUT 1,000 CALORIES
PER SQUARE INCH BUT
TEENAGE BOYS **LOVE IT!**

FOUR EGGS, TWO CUPS SUGAR,
ONE CUP MELTED BUTTER,
1½ CUPS FLOUR, ⅓ CUP
COCOA, 1 TSP VANILLA, ONE
CUP COCONUT, ONE CUP
CHOPPED PECANS, 7 OZ
JAR MARSHMALLOW FLUFF.

ICING: HALF CUP MELTED
BUTTER, 6 TBS. CREAM OR
MILK, ⅓ CUP COCOA, 1 TSP
VANILLA, 1 LB. BOX CON-
FECTIONER'S SUGAR, ONE
CUP CHOPPED PECANS.

MIX EGGS AND SUGAR FOR FIVE MINUTES IN A
MIXER. ADD BUTTER, FLOUR, COCOA, VANILLA,
COCONUT AND PECANS. MIX THOROUGHLY AND POUR
INTO WELL GREASED 9X13" PAN. BAKE AT 350°
FOR 30 MINUTES. WHILE WARM SPREAD WITH
MARSHMALLOW FLUFF. LET SET FOR 20 MINUTES.
MIX ICING INGREDIENTS AND FROST.

NEBRASKA
THRESHER'S
CAKE

THIS CAKE WAS SERVED TO THE TEAMS OF THRESHERS WHO WOULD TRAVEL FROM FARM TO FARM TO BRING IN THE HARVEST IN A TIME BEFORE FARMERS OWNED THEIR OWN EQUIPMENT.

1½ CUP BOILING WATER
ONE CUP ROLLED OATS.
HALF CUP BUTTER
ONE CUP BROWN SUGAR.
ONE CUP SUGAR
FOUR EGGS
1½ CUP FLOUR
ONE tsp. BAKING SODA
ONE tsp. CINNAMON
ONE tsp. NUTMEG
HALF tsp. SALT

POUR BOILING WATER OVER THE OATS. MIX WELL. CREAM BUTTER AND SUGARS. BEAT IN THE EGGS, ONE AT A TIME. STIR IN SOAKED OATMEAL. SIFT DRY INGREDIENTS AND ADD TO BATTER. BAKE IN GREASED 9x13" PAN AT 350° FOR 30-35 MINUTES.

COCONUT PECAN FROSTING.

COMBINE ONE CUP EVAPORATED MILK, ONE CUP BROWN SUGAR, THREE SLIGHTLY BEATEN EGG YOLKS, HALF CUP BUTTER AND ONE tsp VANILLA. COOK STIRRING OVER MEDIUM HEAT UNTIL THICKENED ABOUT 12 MINUTES. ADD 1⅓ CUP FLAKED COCONUT AND ONE CUP CHOPPED PECANS. COOL UNTIL THICK ENOUGH TO SPREAD, BEATING OCCASIONALLY.

Pecan Pie

My Mother in Law, Mary Ann, makes the best pies and this is one of her specialties. She insists on only the freshest nuts.

Mix together all but whole pecans. Pour into unbaked pie shell. Decorate top with whole pecans. Cook for 10 minutes at 375° then up to 50 minutes more at 350°. Begin to check pie after 35 minutes. Pie is done when center does not jiggle.

3 Eggs

½ cup butter softened

1 cup pecans in pie pieces (you can toast for 5 minutes at 350° to bring out the taste of pecans)

Whole pecans for top

½ cup sugar

2 Tbs flour

1 cup light corn syrup

1 tsp. vanilla.

- POUND -
cake

WE CALL THIS JOY'S POUND CAKE.
JOY IS JIM'S FIRST COUSIN AND
beloved by ALL OF US. WHEN OUR
CHILDREN WERE VERY LITTLE, OUR
TWO FAMILIES WENT CAMPING
TOGETHER A COUPLE OF TIMES,
AND JOY ALWAYS HAD ONE OF
THESE POUND CAKES TO WHIP
OUT JUST WHEN WE NEEDED IT
AFTER A LONG BUT JOY FILLED
DAY CHASING TODDLERS AROUND.

- TWO AND ONE FOURTH CUPS FLOUR
- TWO CUPS SUGAR
- HALF tsp. BAKING SODA
- ONE tsp. VANILLA
- ONE CUP BUTTER
- THREE EGGS
- ONE CUP SOUR CREAM.

BEAT ALL INGREDIENTS
TOGETHER FOR THREE
MINUTES WITH AN
ELECTRIC MIXER. POUR
INTO BUTTERED AND
FLOURED BUNDT PAN OR
ANGEL FOOD TIN BAKE
AT 325 DEGREES FOR
ONE HOUR.

TEXAS
SHEET CAKE

ANOTHER POTLUCK STANDBY, THIS CAKE IS EASY TO THROW TOGETHER AND MAKES A MOIST, YUMMY CHOCOLATE CAKE. MIGUEL, WHO IS FROM SAN ANTONIO, TEXAS, MIGHT CALL THIS NEW HAMPSHIRE SHEET CAKE AS HE HAD NEVER HEARD OF IT UNTIL HE MOVED HERE.

TWO STICKS BUTTER, ONE CUP WATER, FOUR Tbs. COCOA, TWO CUPS FLOUR, TWO CUPS SUGAR, HALF tsp. SALT, TWO EGGS, HALF CUP SOUR CREAM, HALF tsp. BAKING SODA.

FOR THE CAKE: BRING BUTTER, WATER AND COCOA TO A BOIL IN A MEDIUM SAUCEPAN. REMOVE FROM HEAT AND ADD FLOUR, SUGAR AND SALT RIGHT TO THE SAUCEPAN. BEAT IN EGGS, SOUR CREAM AND BAKING SODA. BAKE IN A GREASED JELLY ROLL PAN (10 X 15) OR WIDE FLAT PAN WITH A RIM AT 350 DEGREES FOR 20-25 MINUTES. DO NOT OVER COOK.

⊰ FROSTING ⊱

ONE STICK butter, FOUR Tbs. COCOA, SIX Tbs. MILK, ONE lb. box OF CONFECTIONER'S SUGAR, ONE Tsp. VANilla, ONE CUP CHOPPED WALNUTS OR PECANS.

FOR FROSTING: BRING to boil butter, COCOA AND MILK IN that SAME SAUCEPAN. REMOVE FROM HEAT. ADD CONFECTIONER'S SUGAR, VANilla AND NUTS. FROST THE CAKE AS SOON AS POSSIBLE AFTER TAKING it FROM THE OVEN.

☆Teddy's☆
CHOCOLATE PUDDING

TEDDY WOULD MAKE THIS by TOSSING IN FANCY CHOCOLATE BARS. THIS GAVE IT A GLAMOUR NOT OFTEN ASSOCIATED WITH PUDDING.

½ CUP SUGAR
2 Tbs. CORN STARCH
¼ tsp. SALT
1 EGG
2 CUPS MILK
2 SQUARES UNSWEETENED CHOCOLATE (OR IN THE SPIRIT OF TEDDY, WHATEVER CHOCOLATE YOU WANT TO TOSS IN)

BREAK CHOCOLATE INTO PIECES IF YOU CAN. PUT EVERYTHING TOGETHER IN A SAUCEPAN EXCEPT THE BUTTER AND VANILLA. COOK OVER LOW HEAT, STIRRING UNTIL THE MIXTURE COMES TO A BOIL. BOIL ONE MINUTE, STIRRING. BLEND IN ONE Tbs. VANILLA AND ONE Tbs. BUTTER. POUR INTO A HEAT PROOF DISH AND REFRIGERATE. OF COURSE THIS IS GREAT WITH WHIPPED CREAM OR JUST PLAIN CREAM POURED ON IT AND SWIRLED IN AS YOU EAT.

NO, THIS IS NOT A COMMENT ON TEDDY'S PUDDING — FOR MANY YEARS, THERE WAS AN OUTHOUSE BETWEEN OUR HOUSE AND TEDDY'S THAT THE KIDS MADE INTO A FORT — SO THIS OUTHOUSE IS (SORT OF) RELEVANT!

TRES LECHES CAKE

(OR AS WE CALL IT: YESSENIA'S TRA LA LA CAKE)

WHEN YESSENIA ARAYA MESEN WAS GROWING UP IN COSTA RICA, HER MOTHER RAN A BAKERY. THE APPLE DIDN'T FALL FAR FROM THE TREE AS YESSENIA IS ALSO AN AMAZING BAKER. WHILE YESSENIA WORKED HERE, IT WASN'T A STAFF GATHERING WITHOUT ONE OF THESE CAKES ▭ ▭ ▭ ▭ ▭ ▭ ▭

1¼ CUP FLOUR

8 EGGS, ROOM TEMPERATURE

1 tsp. BAKING POWDER

1 CUP SUGAR

1 tsp. VANIIIA

1 CAN SWEETENED CONDENSED MILK

1 CAN EVAPORATED MILK

1 CUP WHIPPING CREAM

¼ CUP RUM

BEAT EGG WHITES UNTIL STIFF. GRADUALLY ADD SUGAR AS FOR AN ANGEL FOOD CAKE. FOLD IN BEATEN YOLKS AND VANIIIA THEN FLOUR. BAKE IN 9×13 INCH PAN - 350° OVEN FOR 20 MINUTES OR SO.

MIX ^RUM AND MIIKS TOGETHER, PUNCH HOLES IN CAKE WITH FORK AND POUR MIIK MIXTURE OVER BAKED CAKE. THEN LEAVE TO SOAK IN REFRIGERATOR.

▭ ▭ ▭ ▭ ▭ ▭ ▭ ▭ ▭

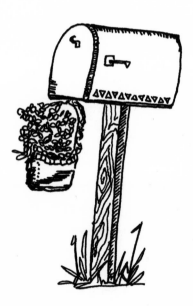

burnt...sugar fudge....

This is Sophie Carden's recipe. She was born in Cornwall, England and lived there until she was ten when her parents, Deb and Ava moved the family to nearby Cornish, New Hampshire. Cornwall has a tradition of great fudge so this recipe was one that Sophie found and made her own when she was looking for a taste of home.

: SIX CUPS SUGAR : TWO CUPS CREAM :
1/4 tsp. baking SODA : HALF cup butter :
ONE Tbs. VANILLA : THREE CUPS NUTS,
CHOPPED (OPTIONAL) :

MIX FOUR CUPS OF SUGAR AND CREAM IN large HEAVY PAN AND BRING TO TO BOIL. PUT REMAINING TWO CUPS OF SUGAR INTO A heavy skillet and place ON LOW HEAT, STIRRING CONSTANTLY UNTIL SUGAR IS completely melted AND LOOKS LIKE brown SUGAR, LIGHT BROWN IN COLOR. WHEN SUGAR IS MELTED POUR INTO FIRST boiling MIXTURE. MIX WELL AND LET COOK UNTIL IT MAKES A FIRM ball When DroppED IN COLD WATER. SET OFF the FIRE AND STIR IN SODA, UNTIL MIXTURE FOAMS. ADD butter and Stir UNTIL MELTED. LET MIXTURE SET FOR 20 MINUTES AND THEN ADD Vanilla AND beAT UNTIL HEAVY. STIR IN NUTS and POUR INTO A buttered PAN. LET COOL AND CUT INTO SQUARES.

FAUX-JITO

"FOR THE DAYS WHEN A
MOJITO IS JUST TOO MUCH." — LOVE, LIZZY

JUICE OF TWO LEMONS AND TWO LIMES
MUDDLE WITH A HANDFUL OF FRESH
MINT LEAVES.

LET SIT FOR A FEW MINUTES.

WHILE YOU WAIT: MAKE A SIMPLE SYRUP
OF ONE CUP SUGAR AND ONE
CUP WATER.
BOIL UNTIL SUGAR DISSOLVES.

ADD TWO PARTS TOGETHER AND
STIR.

SERVE WITH SPARKLING WATER
ON THE ROCKS!

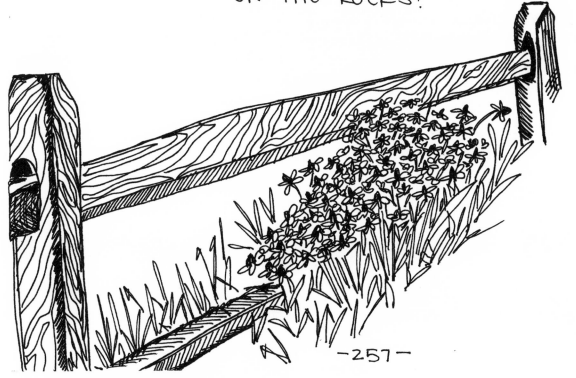

CARAMEL Corn

BEFORE SHE MOVED back to THE MIDWEST WHERE SHE WAS FROM, JESS Miller WORKED At the FARM FOR SEVERAL YEARS. While HERE She got US hooKED ON THIS CARAMEL CORN Which We have KNOWN to Call "CRACK CORN". Jess Also brought OUR Graphics INTO the 21st CENTURY As the technical WIZARD behind ALL the logos We Created FOR EACH COllECTION OF FLOWER ESSENCES. JESS ALSO DESIGNED OUR ANIMAL WELLNESS broChURE, AND HER bELOVED BRODY IS ONE OF THE FEATURED DOGS. SHE CONTINUES to DO ALL OUR POSTCARDS AND REMAINS OUR GRAPhic dESIGNER FOR PROJECTS big AND SMALL.

PLACE 5-6 QUARTS POPPED POPCORN IN A LARGE FOIL PAN (3/4 CUPS OF UNPOPPED CORN = 18 CUPS POPPED)

PARTY?

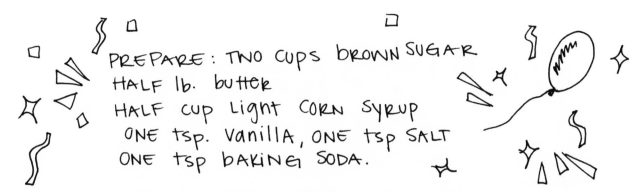

PREPARE: TWO CUPS BROWN SUGAR
HALF lb. butter
HALF cup light CORN SYRUP
ONE tsp. VANILLA, ONE tsp SALT
ONE tsp BAKING SODA.

BOIL BROWN SUGAR, butter AND light CORN SYRUP
FOR FIVE MINUTES, REMOVE FROM HEAT AND ADD
VANILLA, SALT AND BAKING SODA.

BLEND AND POUR OVER POPCORN. FOLD AND MIX
UNTIL EVERYTHING IS COATED. PLACE SINGLE
LAYER ON COOKIE SHEETS LINED WITH PARCH-
MENT PAPER. COOK IN 250 DEGREE OVEN FOR
40 MINUTES. STIR OCCASIONALLY FROM THE
bottom. DRY ON parchment PAPER AND ALLOW
TO COOL.

USING A FOIL ROASTING PAN FOR the MIXING,
BAKING AND COOLING OR A REALLY big bowl
OR PAN helps ESPECIALLY When MAKING MORE
THAN ONE BATCH AT A TIME.

Gingerbread House RECIPE

THIS RECIPE WIll WIN NO PRIZES FOR TASTE but IS EXCELLENT FOR ROll-ING OUT INTO the PIECES FOR A GINGERbREAD HOUSE.

WE OFTEN MAKE THE PIECES FOR A LOT OF LIttLE HOUSES AND LET EVERYONE WHO WANTS to MAKE A HOUSE ASSEMbLE AND DECORATE ONE. AT the end WE HAVE A VIllAGE TO ADMIRE AND EVENTUAlly, TO MUNCH ON.

9 CUPS FLOUR, 1 Tbs LEMON PEEL, 2 tsp. GROUND GINGER, 1/2 tsp. SAlt, 2 CUPS DARK CORN SYRUP, 1 1/4 CUP butter.

CREAM butter AND SUGAR, ADD CORN SYRUP THEN DRY INGREDIENTS. I ROll the SIDE AND ROOF PIECES OUT bETWEEN PARCHMENT PAPER. I SOME-TIMES DON'T ADD ALL THE FLOUR, KEEPING THE DOUGH A LIttLE EASIER to ROll. if it's STICKIER, IT DOESN'T SEEM TO MAtTER SINCE the PAPER KEEPS IT FROM STICKING TO THE ROllING PIN. WE CUT WINDOWS bEFORE bAKING AND Fill THEM WITH CRUSHED LIFE SAVERS.

BAKE AT 350 DEGREES FOR 12-15 MINUTES.

FROSTING: ON ONE OF MY EARLY DATES WITH JIM, HE SPENT THE EVENING HOLDING TOGETHER THE WALLS OF A GINGERBREAD HOUSE FOR ME. THAT WAS BEFORE I DISCOVERED THIS GREAT FROSTING THAT REALLY HOLDS THINGS TOGETHER WELL AND HAS A WONDERFUL OPAQUE AND SNOWY LOOK TO IT.

3 EGG WHITES, 1 box 10x SUGAR, ½ tsp CREAM OF TARTAR, 1 tsp VANILLA.

BEAT ALL INGREDIENTS FOR 7-10 MINUTES.

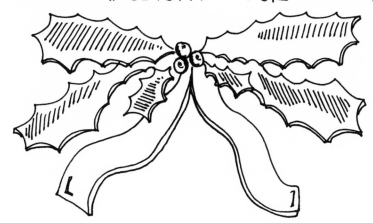

HAPPY HOLIDAYS♡.

PuP C🐾KES and

DOGGIE ICE CREAM

WE LOVE DOGS! IT WOULDN'T BE GREEN HOPE FARM COOKBOOK WITHOUT A COUPLE RECIPES FOR THESE DEAR FRIENDS! THESE TWO RECIPES ARE FROM Alli HOWE WHOSE DOG PACK LOVES HER JUST AS MUCH AS WE DO AND WITH GOOD REASON. THIS WOMAN IS A DOG WHISPERER PAR EXCELLENCE!

PUP CAKES: HALF CUP NATURAL PEANUT BUTTER (NO SUGAR) 1/4 CUP VEGETABLE OIL 🐾 ONE tsp. VANILLA 🐾 1/3 CUP HONEY 🐾 TWO EGGS 🐾 1 1/2 CUPS WHOLE WHEAT FLOUR 🐾 ONE tsp. BAKING SODA 🐾 ONE HEAPING CUP SHREDDED APPLES OR CARROTS 🐾

PUP CAKE FROSTING: 12 OUNCES CREAM CHEESE 🐾 TWO Tbs. WHOLE WHEAT FLOUR 🐾 TWO Tbs. HONEY 🐾 SHREDDED CARROTS AS A GARNISH 🐾

PREHEAT OVEN TO 350 DEGREES. LINE MUFFIN TIN WITH MUFFIN PAPERS. COMBINE PEANUT BUTTER, OIL, VANILLA, HONEY AND EGGS IN A MEDIUM BOWL, MIXING WELL. SIFT FLOUR AND BAKING SODA AND FOLD INTO MIX. ADD CARROTS OR APPLES. BAKE 35-40 MINUTES. BEAT FROSTING INGREDIENTS TOGETHER. FROST THE PUP CAKES THEN GARNISH THEM WITH SHREDDED CARROTS. TO AMP UP THE DOG PARTY CELEBRATION, SERVE WITH DOGGIE ICE CREAM.

DOGGIE ICE CREAM

🐾 TWO BANANAS 🐾 TWO Tbs. PLAIN YOGURT 🐾 TWO Tbs. HONEY 🐾 THREE Tbs. PEANUT butter

BLENDERIZE EVERYTHING THEN FREEZE INTO ICE CREAM by USING AN ICE CUBE TRAY OR CUP CAKE TIN. THIS RECIPE IS REALLY FLEX-IbIe - AMOUNTS CAN be CHANGED, IT CAN be DOUbIED AND IT'S EASY to EMbEIIiSH WITH OTHER INGREDIENTS. AS LONG AS IT HAS PEANUT butter AS AN INGREDiENT, DOGS WILL LOVE IT!

THESE RECIPES ARE IN MEMORY OF AIIi'S DOG ♡OLiVE. LOOK FOR OTHER OLIVE SHOUT OUTS THROUGHOUT THE COOK-bOOK.

MONTEREY JACK
and
Chipotle Cheese Sauce

THIS CAN BE POURED ON CHICKEN, FISH OR SHRIMP.

8 OUNCES CREAM CHEESE, SOFTENED

2 CUPS HEAVY CREAM

1½ tsp. GROUND CUMIN

½ tsp. SALT

¼ CUP PUREED CHIPOTLE CHILES IN ADOBO SAUCE (OR 1-2 Tbs. FOR MILDER SAUCE)

1 Tbs. MINCED GARLIC

2 Tbs. FLOUR

2 CUPS GRATED MONTEREY JACK CHEESE (YOU CAN USE PEPPER JACK OR PLAIN)

¼ CUP FINELY CHOPPED CILANTRO

IN A STURDY SAUCEPAN, WHISK FIRST SEVEN INGREDIENTS TOGETHER OVER MEDIUM HEAT UNTIL MELTED AND SMOOTH. ADD GRATED CHEESE AND STIR UNTIL MELTED. REMOVE FROM HEAT AND STIR IN CILANTRO.

IF USING SAUCE FOR CHICKEN, BAKE IN 350 DEGREE OVEN. FIRST COOK CHICKEN LIGHTLY SEASONED WITH SALT AND PEPPER FOR A HALF HOUR THEN COVER WITH CHIPOTLE SAUCE AND COOK FOR ANOTHER 20 MINUTES. THEN SPRINKLE WITH AN ADDITIONAL CUP OF MONTEREY JACK CHEESE AND COOK AN ADDITIONAL TEN MINUTES.

SANGRIA
a la
BEN

ELIZABETH IS NOT THE ONLY SHEEHAN WHO HAS WALKED THE CAMINO DE SANTIAGO DE COMPOSTELA. BEN ALSO WALKED THE CAMINO IN 2009. AS THE CAMINO WINDS ITS WAY THROUGH THE RIOJA REGION IN SPAIN, BEN LIKES TO MAKE HIS SANGRIA WITH A RIOJA RED WINE FROM THIS AREA. THIS WINE IS CONSIDERED A TRADITIONAL WINE FOR SANGRIA AND ALSO BRINGS BACK END OF A LONG DAY ON THE TRAIL CAMINO MEMORIES.

- 1.5 LITRE OF RED WINE
- ONE CUP BRANDY (BEN USES CALVADOS, AN APPLE BRANDY)
- HALF CUP TRIPLE SEC
- ONE CUP ORANGE JUICE
- ONE CUP POMEGRANATE JUICE (BEN FEELS THIS IS THE KEY INGREDIENT IN THIS RECIPE AND SHOULD NOT BE OMITTED NO MATTER WHAT!)
- HALF CUP SIMPLE SYRUP
- SLICED FRUITS ESPECIALLY ORANGES BUT ADD APPLES TOO IF USING THE CALVADOS.

MIX ALL LIQUID INGREDIENTS THEN ADD THE FRUIT AND REFRIGERATE. YOUR SANGRIA IS READY.

SIMPLE SYRUP

ONE CUP WATER, ONE CUP WHITE SUGAR — COMBINE SUGAR AND WATER IN A SAUCE PAN AND BRING TO A BOIL. ONCE SUGAR HAS DISSOLVED, TAKE THE PAN OFF THE BURNER. ALLOW TO COOL BEFORE USING.

A
TOMATO
chutney

THIS CHUTNEY ADDS
A LOT TO A CHEESE SANDWICH.
WE ALWAYS USED IT WITH LONG
TIME GREEN HOPE FARM STAFF
GODDESS DEB CARDEN'S CORNISH
PASTIES WHEN SHE MADE THEM FOR
THE LOCAL FARMER'S MARKET. IT
IS WORTH TRYING IF YOU HAVE A
GLUT OF TOMATOES AS IT HAS
A VERY INTERESTING TASTE.

THREE lbs RIPE TOMATOES, SKINNED
TWO CUPS SUGAR
1/2 lb SHALLOTS OR ONIONS, CHOPPED
3/4 CUP SULTANAS (RAISINS)
ONE Tbs. SALT
ONE tsp PEPPER
THREE LEVEL tsp. MUSTARD SEED
1/2 tsp. ALLSPICE
3 3/4 CUPS VINEGAR

PUT ALL INGREDIENTS BUT TOMATOES AND
SHALLOTS IN A SAUCEPAN AND BRING TO A
boiL. ADD TOMATOES AND SHALLOTS AND
SIMMER WITHOUT A LID UNTIL THICK
LIKE JAM.

yogi
TEA

this is a wonderful warming winter tea, free of caffeine but full of FLAVOR.

- five cloves
- five peppercorns
- several thin slices of ginger
- one cinnamon stick
- five or more cardamon seeds.

Simmer these five ingredients in two cups of water for about ten minutes. Add half cup cream and simmer for about ten minutes or more.

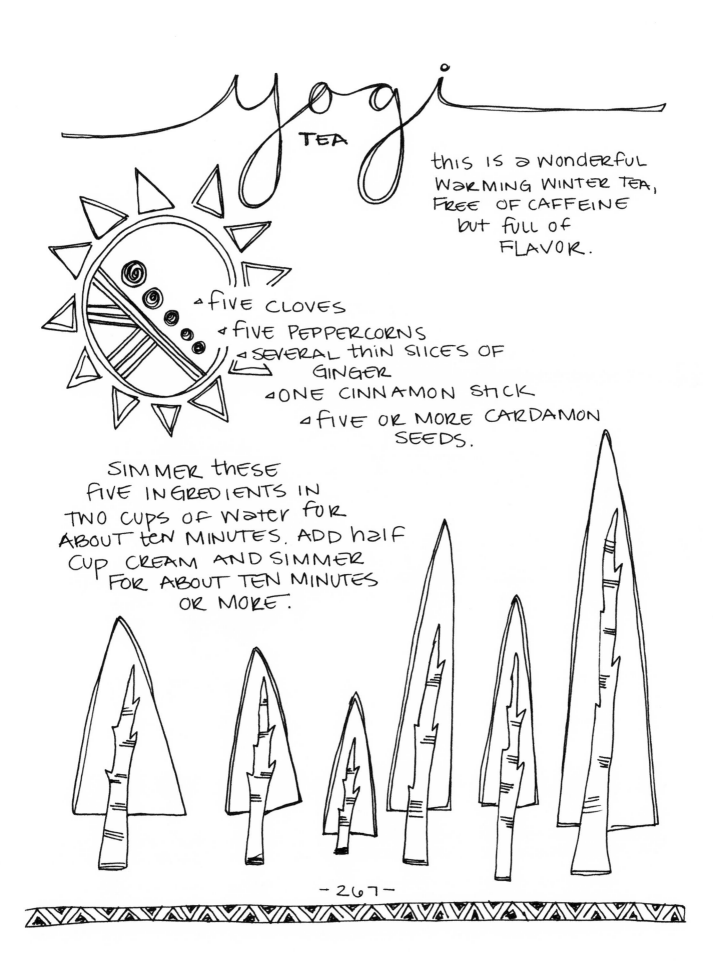

BABA AND CRACKER.